FELT craft

Sue Freeman

FELT
craft

*Hand crafted felt
from fleece to
finished projects*

A DAVID & CHARLES CRAFT BOOK

ACKNOWLEDGEMENTS

John Knight for taking the photographs.

Anna Bowers from 'Fibre Crafts', Style Cottage, Lower Eashing, Godalming, Surrey, for help with supplies and equipment.

Mary Burkett, Abbot Hall Art Gallery, Kendal, Cumbria, for allowing me to use her publication *The Art of the Feltmaker* as a source of historic felt information.

Shirley Simpson from 'Something Sheepey', Ivy House, Dennington Road, Framlington, Woodbridge, Suffolk, for supplying lovely dyes and very comprehensive instructions.

Fran Benton from 'Little London Spinners', House Farm Workshops, East Tytherley Road, Lockerley, Romsey, Hampshire, who supplied superb dyed fleece that is ideal for felt making.

Anne, Julie and Roweena from West Surrey College of Art & Design who provided all kinds of help too numerous to mention, and were responsible for introducing me to felt making.

Sarah Jones helped tremendously with making samples for the book.

Cloe Dancy from 'Orange Court Farm', Littleton, nr Guildford, Surrey, for letting John and myself photograph four of her twenty-eight breeds of sheep.

Carol Connealley for her felt-making technique.

Rosemary Woods for help with typing.

Ewa Kuniczak-Coles for the inspiration behind the washing machine method and for being an excellent secretary of the 'Felt Makers Association', Wilton House, 13 Norfolk Street, Southsea, Portsmouth, Hampshire.

Vivienne Wells for all her encouragement.

(pp 2-3)
A rainbow of dyed fleece – the starting point for feltmaking with colour

British Library Cataloguing in Publication Data

Freeman, Sue, *1959–*
   Felt! – hand-crafted felt – from fleece
   to finished projects.
   1. Handicrafts using felts – Manuals
   I. Title
   746′ .0463

   ISBN 0-7153-9104-6

Typeset by ABM Typographics Ltd, Hull
and printed in West Germany
by Mohundruck GmbH
for David & Charles Publishers plc
Brunel House   Newton Abbot   Devon

Distributed in the United States by
Sterling Publishing Co, Inc,
2, Park Avenue, New York, NY 10016

CONTENTS

Colour Plate 1 Detail of a patchwork quilt showing felt samples sewn together with embroidery stitches in woollen yarn

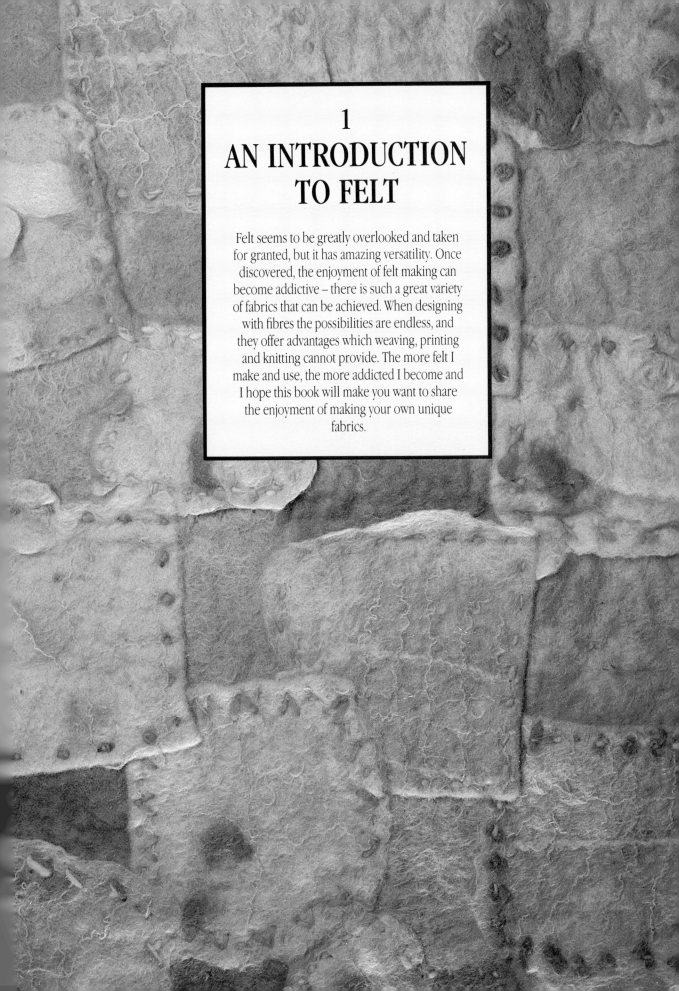

1
AN INTRODUCTION TO FELT

Felt seems to be greatly overlooked and taken for granted, but it has amazing versatility. Once discovered, the enjoyment of felt making can become addictive – there is such a great variety of fabrics that can be achieved. When designing with fibres the possibilities are endless, and they offer advantages which weaving, printing and knitting cannot provide. The more felt I make and use, the more addicted I become and I hope this book will make you want to share the enjoyment of making your own unique fabrics.

WHAT IS FELT?

The most important fact about felt is that it has to be made from wool fibre. Unlike a woven or knitted textile, made from a continuous spun thread of wool fibres, felt is made from the un-spun wool fibres and is therefore known as a fabric rather than a textile.

Wool is the only natural fibre that will felt. In fact, it is the natural quality of wool fibre to felt. When making felt you are providing the correct conditions to help the wool fibres matt together in a controlled manner. Everyone is familiar with accidents that can happen when washing woollen items. A woollen garment will shrink and look matted after too harsh a treatment when washing, because of the structure of the wool fibre.

A close examination of a wool fibre under a microscope reveals why wool will felt naturally. The fibre or staple is constructed by a series of overlapping scales that have a serrated edge. The scales overlap and provide a staple with a pointed tip (see Fig 1). A human hair is quite similar in construction but a wool fibre differs because of its molecular structure. A protein called keratin is present in wool and the molecular structure of keratin protein gives wool elasticity or *creep*. The keratin protein is formed in a spiral formation and, depending on the age of the sheep and

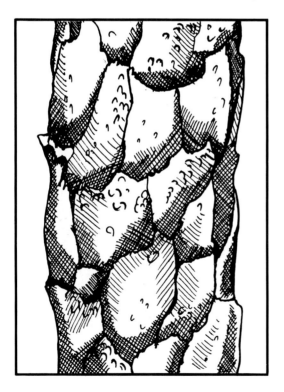

type of fleece, the creep can vary. If one staple of wool fibre is held between two fingers and pulled through against the scales the fibre reacts rather like a spring. So it is the fibre structure and creep that play an important part in making wool fibre felt.

Obviously wool does not felt on its own, otherwise sheep would be walking around in felt jackets, but it does need the action of four elements. These are heat, moisture, friction and pressure. When the wool fibres are exposed to these four elements, the scales on the staple open up and the creep makes them tangle. The more they are exposed to these conditions the tougher the felt. As the fibres begin to dry the creep shrinks back and the serrated edges catch onto other fibres and produce a mesh of fibres which of course is felt.

The simple way wool felts perhaps explains a little of its versatility when designing with wool fibres. Your hands are all that are required to provide the warmth, moisture, friction and pressure needed to felt wool fibre.

THE ORIGINS OF FELT

Legend tells that one day St Christopher set out on a long journey. He had walked for many miles and had grown weary so he decided to stop and rest for a while. He found a good shady spot under a tree and sat down and removed his sandals to soothe his feet. Whilst he was relaxing, he had an idea. St Christopher had noticed some fleece caught on bushes from passing sheep so he gathered several handfuls and lined his sandals. He now felt refreshed to continue his journey and now his sandals were far more comfortable from the fleece that cushioned his feet. Eventually he reached his journey's end and removed his sandals to wash his feet. As he took off his sandals, he was amazed to find that the sheeps' fleece had turned into a fabric. This, of course, was felt.

It is possible that felt was discovered, quite by accident, in a similar way to this. It is the oldest form of controlled fabric made by man and pre-dates Christianity. Prehistoric man hunted animals for food and used the animal skins to clothe himself and sleep on. The mixture of body weight, heat, movement and perspiration would have created the ideal conditions for felting the skins. Once it was noticed what was happening to the fibres it was then possible to control this and make felt as an intended fabric.

The oldest and finest felt remains that have been found date from around 700BC. These remains were found in very good condition in the frozen tombs at Pazyryk in the Atlai mountains in Siberia. The tombs belonged to a nomadic tribe of horsemen. Due to the

Fig 2 A typical ethnic felt tent

frozen conditions the remains were in excellent condition and the variety of items found made from felt showed how extensively it was used by these people. They made their tents from felt, as well as their clothes and decorations for their animals, including saddles. One very interesting observation from this civilization (700–200BC), is that nearly all the felt was patterned. Being a nomadic tribe these people herded animals which had to serve many purposes. The sheep they herded would supply food and milk products as well as fabric. It appears that this tribe was illiterate but very advanced with its craft skills. These people decorated their felt with animal symbols: most commonly used were swans, cockerels, rams, goats, deer and lions. They also depicted mythical creatures like the griffin and the dragon. This tribe travelled along the main trading routes between East and West and as a result felt making spread to other countries.

It is the many unique properties of felt which give it advantages over other textiles and explain why these people used felt extensively throughout their daily lives. Their tents were strong enough to resist the wind and rain and snowy conditions. Their many layers of felt clothing and bedding would insulate them against the elements. It is also known that ancient man made his armour from layers of thick felt and leather as it was dense enough to resist fire and arrowheads.

In Iran, the nomadic tribes still make their portable homes from felt. They probably don't vary much in de-

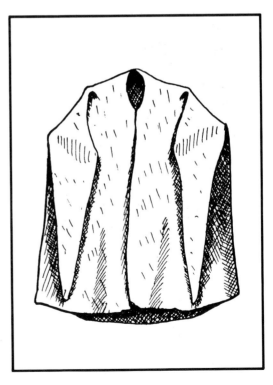

Fig 3 A shepherd's cloak or kepenak

9

sign and principle from the Pazyryk nomads' tents. The tents are made from a structure of poles and then covered over with large sheets of felt that are tied on (see Fig 2). The advantage of using felt is that the homes are portable and felt is not affected by changes in climate. Due to the density of the fabric, snow and rain cannot penetrate nor can extremes of temperature crack or destroy the felt. Such tents are very large and are all hand made. Despite the strenuous activity involved in making such large pieces, the task of felt making is quite often undertaken by women.

In Turkey the old tradition of making *kepenaks* or cloaks and using them still exists. These garments look decidedly ancient because of their design and it is doubtful this has changed very much, if at all, over the centuries. The purpose of a kepenak is to keep the shepherd warm, dry and comfortable (see Fig 3). The unusual thing about this garment is its shape. It is made from one piece of felt only and although the kepenak has the suggestion of sleeves, rather like an animal in mid stages of evolution, they are in fact not intended for use. The kepenak is made from very stiff rough natural-coloured fleece and acts as a personal tent for the shepherd when he needs shelter.

FELT FOR HATS

Felt has always been a popular material for making hats and still is. Hats demonstrate the versatility of the felt structure. The crimp in the staple gives the felt elasticity and therefore makes it relatively easy to mould.

We only need to study the history of fashion and observe drawings and portraits to discover how popular hats have always been. A stone engraving found this century at Housesteads on Hadrian's Wall depicts three figures in hooded cloaks believed to have been made from felt because they resemble the kepenak. In 1867 in the Lake District some felt hoods found in the peat were in a similar style to the hoods worn by the three figures.

In medieval times hats were quite commonly made from beaver and rabbit fur. Today rabbit fur is still used for felt in hat making but the process of making fur felt is very different to wool felt. A fur fabric is different in structure to a wool staple. It is necessary to remove the kemp hairs or guard hairs which are the tough fibres from the rabbit fur. Then the fur has to be treated with ammonia to open up the scales and for the barbed tip to link to other fibres. Workers had to handle mercury in the fur felt-making process which often led to madness. Hence the saying 'mad as a hatter'.

The wool for felt hats has to be a very high quality

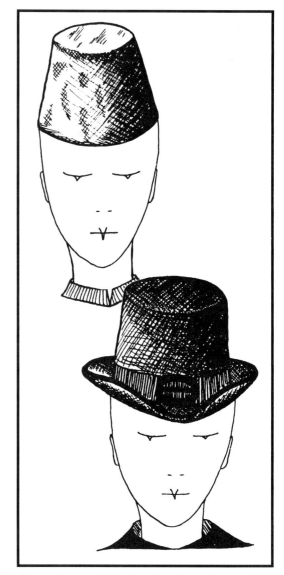

Fig 4 Felt hats: typical ethnic hat or fez, and the early top hat

and therefore is not mixed with a percentage of synthetic fibres. In some parts of Iran it is still possible to see simple hats being made by hand in the traditional method. Unfortunately, most of the felt made originally in Turkey and Iran by traditional hand methods is now being made on industrial machines. This is partly due to tourist demand of felt items.

For a manufactured wool felt hat, the felt used may be cut from a flat sheet or made into a cone ready to be blocked on a hat form. In the felt hat industry, two properties of felt are the most useful – the elasticity of the fabric to be stretched and moulded and the fact that the felt can be made in one piece in the shape of a cone for relatively easy shaping on the hat block.

INDUSTRIAL FELT

Felt is used very widely in industry. One of its main advantages is its durability. Felt hammers are made from very dense felt. This felt has been milled for a long time and therefore becomes very hard and dense, although still lightweight. A felt hammer is very hard wearing, makes less noise, and will not cause problems when being used with metal components, such as sparking and wearing down of metal. In industry felt is also used for filters. Made to the correct specifications of density and with a percentage of synthetic fibres, a felt filter will trap unwanted purities. One ideal use of industrial felt is in polishing machines. Large discs of dense felt are made and then cut to the size of the machine they are to fit. It is particularly important that there are no impurities in the wool fibre blend as these may scratch the surface of the item being polished.

Some very crude felts are made from using a mixture of different wools. These felts are used for padding because felt helps prevent vibration. The felt is used to line the cases that carry large heavy items which need insulating and cushioning in transit. The musical instrument industry also makes use of felt, particularly in piano manufacturing. There are 85 pads, one for each key, inside the piano and these felt key pads play a very important role in producing the sound of the piano, therefore affecting its tone and quality.

FELT IN THE HOME

If we look around our homes we can find many examples of felt. We must, however, be careful not to confuse felt with heavily milled woven fabrics as some materials look very much like felt at first glance, but on closer inspection the warp and weft structure of the woven fabric can be seen. To produce such a material the fibre content has to be mainly wool. Although the wool fibre has been spun, the fibres still react like the unspun wool fibre. Hence during the milling process the overlapping yarn becomes very tightly interlocked. This makes the woven material much denser but with a smooth and slightly fluffy surface. This would be an advantage because the woven material would become harder wearing and warmer due to the closed weave.

Carpet felt is used in the home. This type of felt will be either under the woven tufted carpet to add extra insulation and longer life to the carpet or as a decorative floor covering in itself. Roof felt is used in the loft. This felt is made from mainly synthetic fibres and treated to be water and fire resistant and therefore doesn't really look like felt at all. In furnishings, particularly upholstery, felt is used for padding. Used to cover the springs and stuffing, the felt makes an ideal smooth surface over which to fit the furnishing fabric.

Turkish felt rugs are exported and can be bought alongside tufted or woven carpets. These rugs make very good decoration for walls. If your home is very old, has very uneven walls and is badly insulated, a wall hanging made from felt can be very beneficial. The felt hanging will keep out draughts, keep down noise and cover any imperfections that are difficult to hide. Used as a bed covering, a felt bedspread is light but warm. Of course, if the felt is patterned it has a decorative use as well. One of the big advantages of having felt in the home is that it can be made fire resistant. Because of its construction and density, it is a very difficult fabric to burn. The other advantage of wool fibre is that it will not flare up and give off toxic fumes, unlike a synthetic fibre – a notorious hazard in the home.

In Scandinavia, home crafts are very popular. It is a popular pastime for Scandinavian women to knit or weave on a loom at home. Felt making also is an old Scandinavian home craft that hasn't entirely died out and, with the growing interest in contemporary felt, is now seeing a revival. It was a tradition for felt to be made in the home to produce items for warmth necessary in the sub-zero temperatures of winter. The garments commonly made were mittens, socks and hats. The more accomplished felt maker would make waistcoats and boots. These felt garments were made from natural coloured fleeces that were untreated chemically. The mittens, socks and hats were very often made in one piece with no seams and a little hand embroidery to finish off the garment. Thick felt boots are perfect for dry sub-zero snowy weather conditions. The feet are well insulated against the cold, it is difficult for the snow or moisture to soak through, but at the same time the feet can breathe (see Fig 5).

Fig 5 A pair of Scandinavian boots

During and after World War I, Norwegians made their living from making felt boots. For those living in rural areas, this industry was ideal, as the wool from their sheep was at hand and therefore they did not need to go elsewhere for work. Originally, these boots were made by hand and needed to be stitched at the heel. Later, they were made on a last and therefore needed no stitching. This method is still used today.

CRAFT FELT

The felt that most people are familiar with is the craft felt that can be bought from most haberdashers and craft shops. This felt is produced in many colours and at the cheapest price possible. The felt is made from a blend of wool and viscose and that is why it looks, feels and handles differently to 100 per cent wool felt. The minimum content of wool is approximately 30 per cent, which is why its appearance is rather shiny. It doesn't fray when cut and is easy to sew, staple or nail to a backboard and makes a good smooth surface.

For children it is an ideal fabric because it is safe, cuts easily and can be stuck down with glue. Craft felt is ideal for making stuffed toys, animals and dolls. The felt surface is smooth enough to be able to draw on details such as facial features. For the hand-embroiderer, felt can be used as a background or cut and appliquéd as part of the pattern. Craft felt is very popular for making gifts and small decorations and there is no reason why your own hand-made felt cannot be used in the same way.

STARTING FELT MAKING

Perhaps now you feel you know more about felt than you imagined possible. It is so versatile, but yet so underestimated. The fact that it is relatively easy to make your own felt is an added bonus. You are also in control of the fabric from the beginning to the end. Anyone can make it, from children to adults. You do not need sophisticated equipment or art-school training or an ability to draw and design. If you like playing with fabrics and fibres and making things for yourself you will enjoy felt making and then maybe like myself you will become totally addicted.

TIPS FOR THE BEGINNER

If you have not made felt before, do not set your aims too high to start with. Small items made from felt can be just as charming and satisfying as large ones. There is nothing more disappointing than embarking on a large project not having done your groundwork. Whether you are working by hand or machine, the better you are prepared, the better your finished product. The more organised you are about your design and the way you prepare your fleece the less mistakes you will make and the more time you will save in the long run. However, you can sometimes learn from your mistakes. From one mistake you can discover another interesting aspect of felt making and then use it to your advantage. To start with, it is best to use natural-coloured fleeces and find the type of fleece you like best. Making felt is a personal thing and the more you make, the more aware you will become of what you prefer to use and how and where you prefer to make it. There are plenty of ideas in this book to keep you occupied for a long time, but no doubt you will have good ideas of your own. Think of this book as your guideline and refer to it for useful information, inspiration and advice.

FELT MAKING TODAY

Although felt making is an ancient craft, both hand-made or patterned felt is currently enjoying a revival. More people are getting to know about felt and what to know how to make it. Gradually more textile students are concentrating on felt-making techniques and producing a range of items from articles of clothing to soft sculptures.

The Felt Association has been established for several years now and each year the numbers of members grows. There are always lots of knitters, spinners, weavers and printers, but felt makers are still relatively small in number. The Felt Association newsletter keeps its members from all over the world in touch with current felt-making trends. It lists forthcoming exhibitions, tells you where to buy materials, gives tips on the felt-making process and who is doing what with felt and where. Next time you go to an exhibition, craft fair or museum, look out for the felt items. Perhaps you will look at them with a fresh eye now that you know what felt is. Who knows, you may end up exhibiting your own work.

I trust by now that you are bursting with enthusiasm to start making your own felt. Decide where you are going to make it, sort out your materials, follow the instructions in this book and see where your felt making will lead you.

Happy Felt making!

2
THE CRAFT KIT

If you have not made felt before, then you will
need to know what equipment is required, what
materials are needed and where to buy them. A
very important consideration is where you
are going to make your felt. Once you are clear
on these points, you will be ready to start
making your own felt. Then all you need to
do is follow the step-by-step guide in
Chapter 3.

THE FLEECE

What fleece to use

Read through the list of types of fleece and their description (see page 16). Then when you go to buy your fleece, you will choose one that is suitable for felting or relatively easy to use. It is important to find the right fleece so that your first attempt at felt making is made as easy as possible whilst you master the various stages.

Where to buy your fleece

There are several places you can purchase fleeces from. You may be lucky and have a local sheep farm nearby which will be able to supply you. There are a few people who keep specialised breeds of sheep on a small scale and it may be worth asking if they will sell you a fleece. Due to the growing interest in crafts, you may be fortunate and have a craft shop in your town. They may well sell fleece or at least suggest where you will be able to buy some. Alternatively, if you know of a Guild of Craftsmen or a Spinners' and Weavers' Association, ask a member, who will probably know of a supplier and perhaps someone who makes felt. It is possible to obtain most information you will need about suppliers from your telephone directory.

How much fleece and what type

When you start making felt, you will probably want to buy only small amounts of different types of fleece. Therefore, unless you know you can use a whole fleece, you are better off buying approximately 250g (8oz) of each type until you decide which one you prefer. You may be baffled at first, trying to decide which type to buy. Fleece can be bought in two forms. You may be offered the choice of untreated fleece or scoured fleece. If you are buying fleece from a farm, it is quite likely the fleece will be untreated – that is unwashed and not sorted.

If you buy a whole, untreated fleece, or a part of it, you should bear in mind that the quality of the fleece varies from one area to another. Ideally, you want the best areas for felt making. Imagine the fleece on the sheep's back; obviously certain areas get more wear because they are more exposed. These areas will be harsher and more matted or tangled. The softest area will be found under the chin, the stomach and the inside of the tops of the legs. If you buy a whole fleece, it is worth taking time to divide the fleece into piles of different quality. Then use the different areas to make separate pieces of felt. That way, you will see what a difference it can make.

If you are offered scoured or carbonised fleece this will have been sorted, washed and the debris re-

✂ **Plate 1** Unprepared fleece: (left) Deep Kent; (right) Cashmere

✂ **Plate 2** Prepared fleece: (left) mixed fibres; (right) Alpaca sliver

moved. Also, it will probably have been carded, so may be in sliver form, which looks like lengths of hair. Alternatively, it may look more like cotton wool, depending on how it was carded. It is easier to use the treated prepared fleece, because it cuts out one of the preparation stages.

When choosing your fleece, it is worth taking into consideration the length of the staple and the count.

✂ **Colour Plate 2** Felt-making equipment

Jacob

Surrey

Plates 3-6 Sheep with fleece suitable for felting:

Name of Fleece	Count	Staple Length	Handle	Colour
Cheviot	48/54s	7–13cm	Soft	Good
Deep Kent	46/48s	18cm	Reasonably soft	Good
Dorset Horn	56/54s	7–10cm	Crisp	Fairly good
Fine Masham	50s	20cm	Soft	Off-white
Jacob	48/54s	13–20cm	Fairly soft	Piebald
Kent Half Bred	56/58s	5–10cm	Soft	Creamy
Leicester	48s	18–21cm	Soft	Fairly good
Lincoln	36/46s	18–25cm	Hard	Off-white
Merino	60/70s	5–10cm	Soft	Off-white
Merino/Cross	58/60s	5–15cm	Soft	Off-white
North Down	56/58s	6–12cm	Soft	Off-white/little grey
North Leicester	48/50s	23–25cm	Fairly soft	Fairly good
Orkney Native	50/56s	2–12cm	Soft	Off-white, dark grey, brown and black
Ripon Hog	46/48s	23–31cm	Smooth	Very good
Shetland Cross	50/56s	2–12cm	Soft	Off white
Shetland Moorit	56/58s	2–6cm	Soft and silky	Brown
Shetland White	56/58s	2–5cm	Soft and silky	Off-white
Short Super Kent	54s	6–8cm	Soft	Off-white
Shropshire Lamb	56/58s	1–3cm	Soft	Fairly good
South Down	58/60s	2–5cm	Soft	Creamy
Suffolk	56s	10-12cm	Soft	Creamy
Swaledale	48/56s	12–18cm	Reasonably soft	Fairly good

This is only a specimen of fleeces. There are many other types. This will give you a guide for selecting a fleece of a high count and good quality. Long staple fleeces can be cut to shorter lengths.

Shetland

Lincoln Blackface

Ideally, for felt making, you want a short staple (that is, fibre length) and a high count (the fineness and softness of the fibre). The preferred length of staple is approximately 2.5cm (1in) and a count of about 60. The lower the count, the coarser the fibre, and therefore more difficult to felt. The higher the count, the easier it is to felt. A count of 50 to 70 is best (see fibre chart as a guideline). It is worth experimenting with different length staples and counts. You may find you prefer a coarser felt to a finer one. You can always cut the length of the staple to make it shorter.

EQUIPMENT

Equipment needed
- *Undyed fleece (see detailed list of types)*
  - *Carders*
- *Calico or canvas (you could use old sheets)*
  - *Scissors*
  - *Needle and thread*
  - *Kettle*
  - *Soap or acid*
  - *Rolling pin*
  - *Apron*
  - *Rubber gloves*
  - *Wellingtons*
  - *Wooden board*

Carders

Your carders are very beneficial and essential if you are using untreated fleece. The function of the carders is to remove tangles and dirt from the fleece. After carding, the fleece is in an organised state, and all the wool fibres lie in a parallel fashion. When you start making felt, hand carders are adequate. If you start making a lot of felt, it may be worth investing in a drum carder. Hand carders are used by spinners, and you may be able to buy them through your fleece supplier or craft shop. You may be offered a variety of designs of hand carder. They are mainly designed either flat or curved. Generally, the curved design is easier to use, but you may find you prefer the flat ones. They also vary a great deal in price. If you buy the cheapest ones, they may do the job of carding adequately, but not last so long as a more expensive pair.

A drum carder does the same work of the hand carders, but on a much larger scale. A drum carder really does save time when you are making lots of felt or larger pieces. They vary in price slightly and in design. If at all possible, it is a good idea to see one working before you purchase one.

Calico or canvas

The purpose of this material is to protect your carded fleece during the wet stage of felt making. Canvas is good because it has a textured surface, and therefore creates more friction. Calico is also suitable, but if you do not have either, then old sheets or tablecloths, or any similar-weight cotton material could be used to start with. The cloth is re-usable, but you will need to cut it to the size of the piece of felt you are making.

Scissors

You will want to use your scissors whilst preparing your fleece, and when making the felt. It is useful to keep them near you all the time. You will need to cut your canvas or cotton to the size you require. If you are using slivers or a long staple fleece, you will have to cut the fibres to an even length. Once you have carded the fleece, you may want to trim the edges of your carded layers. At the wet stage, it will be necessary to cut open the calico covering and perhaps remove tatty edges.

Needle and thread

The needle and thread are mainly necessary at the preparation stage, but will also be useful at the wet stage if you discover a fault or hole. When making patterned felt, you will need to secure the pattern by sewing through the carded layers.

Kettle

If there is an electric kettle at hand, then this is an excellent way of boiling your water at the wet stage. If it is an automatic kettle that turns off when the water has boiled, that is a big advantage as it means you can keep the kettle topped up with boiling water. If you do not have an electric kettle, then an ordinary kettle or saucepan heated by other means can be used. For safety reasons remember not to use electrical equipment near the area where you are wetting the felt as there will be a lot of surplus water about. If you prefer, it is possible to use hot water straight from the tap. If there are children around then this would be a much safer method.

Soap or acid

To assist with the felting process, at the beginning of the wet stage you may want to use soap or acid. This isn't absolutely necessary, but it is worth experimenting with. Try using nothing, then soap, and then acetic acid, and see what difference it makes. If you decide to use soap, do not use too much, otherwise your fleece will end up a sudsy, slippery mess, and will be detrimental to your piece of felt. If you are using soap, it is necessary to use it in a liquid form. Soap flakes can be made into liquid by mixing with hot water. Alternatively, you could use a liquid soap that you can buy for washing woollen garments. If you want to experiment with acetic acid, do not use too much – it is not necessary to soak the fleece with acid. Acetic acid is white vinegar and can be bought from grocers. Fleece is naturally slightly acidic, and does react better with acid. The smell of the acid is not very pleasant, and although acetic acid is relatively mild, it is necessary to be careful not to get it in the eyes or on the skin. It is advisable not to use acid when making felt with children.

Rolling pin

It is possible to use a wooden rolling pin or cylinder of smooth, hard wood. It is necessary to use the rolling pin towards the end of the wet stage. For small pieces of felt, a domestic rolling pin is suitable, but when making larger pieces, you will need a cylinder of wood that is larger and wider. It is important that your rolling pin is made from wood, as this will produce more friction and will not slip. It will also retain the heat from the hot water.

Apron, rubber gloves and wellingtons

Whilst carding the fleece, it will be necessary to protect your clothes from dirt and debris that will be discarded. At the wet stage, you will need to protect your clothes, hands and feet from hot water as well as from fibres, soap or acid. Therefore it is better to wear an apron made from waterproof material. Rubber gloves are essential to protect your hands from boiling water and acid. The fleece is covered in water for most of the felt-making process, and therefore the rubber gloves will prevent sore and chapped hands. It is a good idea to wear wellingtons to protect your feet from hot water as well as keeping them dry. At the hardening stage, your wellingtons are very useful because you can stamp on your felt instead of using your hands for additional pressure.

Wooden board

It is worth procuring a portable surface for felt-making activities. Very often modern kitchen or bathroom surfaces are not ideal for making felt, as they are too slippery and do not retain heat. An ideal surface is a wooden board made from hardwood, but it must be smooth with no splinters. The board is a very useful piece of equipment because it can be used at many stages. When making the carded layers, they can be placed on to the wooden board for ease of transport to the wet-stage area. It is an ideal surface to work on at the hardening and milling stage. Also, when you have completed your piece of felt, it can be pinned on to the board and left to dry.

WHERE TO MAKE FELT

Once you have assembled the equipment, you will need to decide where you are going to make your felt. It is important to remember the amount of water you will be using, and therefore you will need good drainage. Also, when working with fibres, it is important to realise that they do fly around and travel with the water. Although the fibres are clean, it is a good idea to keep them away from food. Look around your living accommodation, and decide where is the best place to make your felt. The kitchen sink can be ideal for making small pieces of felt, that are no bigger than the size of the base of your sink, and the draining board can help drain away the cold water. You may find the bathroom is a better environment. It may be possible to use the bath, or perhaps the shower tray. The slope of the bath or shower tray should provide fairly good draining.

MAKING FELT OUTSIDE

You may decide not to use either of these rooms, and prefer to make your felt outside. This is quite possible, and can be very enjoyable if the weather is good. If you decide to make your felt outside, then it will be necessary to provide a clean area. The clean area will ensure you keep dirt and grit away from your clean fleece. One way to create a clean area is to set up a table and cover it with plastic sheets, and then place your wooden board on this. Set the table at an angle, and that way the water will drain away. Be sure to angle the table so that the water drains away from you. Alternatively, you could use a tray or bowl the same size as your piece of felt, or a little bigger. If you choose to use a tray or bowl, you could easily make the felt inside or outside for the hardening stage, but at the milling stage or rolling stage you will need another surface.

If you decide to make felt outside, you may prefer to make it on your board on the ground, and then kneel to make it. It may be worth trying out the different options and then decide which place suits you best. It is worth bearing in mind the height you prefer to work at. Making felt leaning over the bath can be very hard on the back. Also, if you decide to stamp on the felt at the hardening stage your bath or shower may not be strong enough. Obviously you have to use your commonsense. When reading through Chapter 3 which deals with the different stages of felt making in detail the most suitable place will probably come to mind.

3
MAKING FELT FOR THE FIRST TIME

Before you start to make your felt, check that
you have all the equipment and materials
you need as outlined in Chapter 2.

PREPARING THE FLEECE

Depending on the type of fleece you have chosen to use, you may have to wash it. If you have bought a scoured fleece, tops or slivers, you will not need to do this. Remember if you have an untreated fleece, straight from the sheep's back, it will be full of dirt, twigs and maybe insects.

Washing

If you have a fleece that needs to be washed, the first thing to do is to remove any visible debris. Then take your fleece and place it in a bowl or sink or lukewarm water. If you do put it straight into hot or boiling water, it may matt and become very tangled. Squeeze it gently and lift it out, and lastly place it in hot, but not boiling, soapy water and leave it to soak for at least one hour. By putting the fleece through a gradual change of water temperature, it will not become unneccessarily tangled, which would make teasing and carding more difficult.

When the fleece is in the hot soapy water, squeeze it gently and move it around frequently. Use a generous amount of soap, but not too much so that you end up with a vat of soap suds. You can either use soap flakes made into a liquid or a liquid soap suitable for washing woollen garments. The soap helps to remove the dirt but the water actually cleans the dirt away. By squeezing the fleece and moving it around, you will release the dirt. The debris will float to the surface of the water, therefore remove this when necessary.

Rinsing

Once you are satisfied that the fleece has soaked for long enough to remove the dirt, and particularly if the water is cold, then it is time to rinse the fleece. As you remove the fleece from the dirty water, gently squeeze it, removing excess water. If the water is still hot, rinse it in hot, then warm, and then cold water. If the water is tepid, then rinse in lukewarm and then cold. It is important to handle the fleece gently when it is wet, as it becomes very heavy. The less you tangle it when it is wet, the less lumpy it will be when dry, and the easier it will be to tease and card. To help to remove it from the water, scoop the fleece out with a colander or sieve. Alternatively, take handfuls out at a time and place in rinsing water. Keep rinsing the fleece until the water is clean and free of soap. If the fleece still looks very dirty, then repeat the whole washing procedure.

Drying

Before you start carding the fleece, it must be completely dry. The fleece is quite delicate when it is wet, therefore you must not handle it harshly as you will break the staple. To help the fleece dry more quickly, you can put it in a pillow case or a calico bag with plenty of room for the fleece to move, and then put it in the spindryer. This removes the excess water quickly, and doesn't damage the fleece or the spindryer, as it is protected by the material. If you do not have a spindryer, then squeeze as much water as you can from the fleece.

To dry the fleece, remove from the cotton bag and put it somewhere airy and warm. It must not be put near a direct heat, for example, on top of radiators or near a naked flame, but somewhere where warm air circulates. If there is nowhere suitable inside, then keep the fleece in the pillow case or cotton bag, and hang it outside to dry. While the fleece is drying, keep turning it so it dries evenly. Only when it is dry can you go on to the next stage. If you want to dye the fleece (see Chapter 5), again, it must be dry.

Teasing or untangling the fleece

If you have bought fleece in the scoured form or slivers, you will not need to tease it, and therefore you can go straight into the carding stage. Fleece that has just been washed and dried will need teasing.

Plate 7 Teasing the fleece

Teasing untangles matted fibres and removes knots and any remaining dirt and debris by gently pulling the fibres apart. To tease, take a good handful of fleece in one hand. Then, with the other hand, pull a few fibres at a time with your finger and thumb. Work quickly but gently through the handful. Debris and dirt will fall out as you separate the fibres. The effect of teasing will make the fleece look very light and fluffy, and also increase its volume. It is very important to tease the fleece well; not only does it make carding easier, but also makes a difference to the finished piece of felt.

CARDING THE FLEECE

Carding combs the fleece, removing any remaining debris and also organising the fibres in a parallel fashion. If you are using slivers, you will not need to card your fleece, but you can if you really want to. Quite often the fibres in sliver form are rather long, perhaps longer than the width of your carders. If this is so, then cut the staple to approximately 2in (4cm) if you want to card it. If you are using slivers and want to make felt with a long fibre, follow the method for building the layers (page 22).

Hand carding

To card your fleece with hand carders, you should first of all mark your carders *left* and *right*, and always use them in these hands respectively. Due to the action of carding, the two hands act differently, use different amounts of pressure and pull at a certain angle that affects the wire teeth. If you are right-handed, start by placing a good handful of fleece on to your left-hand carder. To do this, pull the fibres across the metal teeth from the handle edge to the outer edge. The fibres will catch onto the metal teeth. Place a good handful onto the carders, but do not overfill. Remove any surplus that hasn't caught into the metal teeth. Then with your right-hand carder in your right hand, place squarely on top of the left-hand carder in your left hand. The handles will be pointing outwards away from each other. Keep the left carder steady and pull the right carder evenly across the left one. Repeat this movement several times until the fleece looks flat, and is lying parallel between the metal teeth.

By now, the fleece will be on both carders, and to be able to remove it you must place all the fleece on to one carder. To do this, take your left-hand carder in your left hand with the teeth facing upwards and handle facing towards you. Take the right-hand carder in your right hand with teeth facing down-

Plate 8 Carding with hand carders

wards and handle towards you. Place the handle edge of the right-hand carder onto the outside edge of the left-hand carder. Then pull the right-hand carder across the left one towards yourself. Repeat this movement gently and smoothly, and you should be left with all the fibres on the left-hand carder. To remove the carded layer, ease the fibres on the outside edge and gently pull away the carded layer by lifting upwards from the metal teeth. This will remove the fibres and leave you with one carded layer. If the fibres still look tangled, repeat again. If you are left-handed, follow the same procedure and swap the left- and right-hand movements accordingly.

You will probably have to experiment with how much fleece you put on the carders. You may well find you have to put more or less on next time. It is important that each carded layer is the same thickness to be able to produce a uniform piece of felt.

Drum carding

Using a drum carder is a lot easier. The drum carder generally consists of two narrow-width cylinders through which the teased fleece is fed. One of these two cylinders has small teeth like the hand carder and the other has coarser teeth that are spaced further apart. The one with large teeth is the feeder, and the one with finer teeth starts the combing, and feeds onto the large drum covered with tiny metal teeth. As the fleece is gradually fed through the first two cylinders, the large drum becomes full of parallel fibres. The

Plate 9 **Plate 9** Carding with a drum carder

cylinders are operated by a series of cogs that are rotated by a hand-operated handle. When the large drum is full, the handle will not move very easily. To remove the carded fleece there is a line on the large drum where the teeth end. Cut across this line through the layer of fibres, then, as with the hand carders, ease the fleece away from the teeth and rotate the drum as you go until the whole layer has been removed. It is necessary to experiment with the thickness of the layer and it is important to keep the layers uniform in weight and thickness.

BUILDING THE LAYERS OF FLEECE

There are two alternative ways to build the layers. Either you can card all the fleece first, or card a layer as you lay out your carded fleece. First decide how large a piece of felt you want to make. Bear in mind where you are going to make it. If you have not made felt before, start by making a small piece. A good size to start with is approximately 23cm (9in) square. That size will be roughly three hand-carded layers side by side. If you are using a drum carder, make it to the size of lap or layer. Now take a piece of calico, canvas or cotton that is twice the size in length of your decided measurement and once of the width, but also allowing 8cm (3in) all round. For example, if your piece of felt is going to measure 23cm (9in) square, then cut your cotton to 61 x 38cm (24 x 15in).

Method

Place your calico, canvas or cotton on a flat surface – your wooden board would be ideal. Smooth the cotton flat, place three carded layers side by side facing in the same direction (see Plate 10). For a drum-carded lap, lay it across one half of the piece of cotton. For the second layer, place three carded laps at 90° to the first three, but squarely on top. Do the same with a drum-carded layer. With hand-carded layers, it may be necessary to overlap the laps lying side by side slightly to avoid gaps. For the third layer, place in the same direction as the first, and the fourth the same as the second. Build the layers up until you achieve the thickness you desire, being sure alternate layers are at 90° to the previous one.

How many layers?

To help you decide how many layers you should build up, compress the layers between finger and thumb to see how thick each feels. Depending on what you want to make, this will determine how many layers you use. As a guideline to start with, try five layers. Then next time, use less or more as desired. An additional test for thickness and evenness is to carefully lift your layers up towards the light, and if the light shines through, you will know there is a gap or your layers are not dense enough. If there is a gap, fill it with a blob of fleece. This way it is possible to avoid holes in the finished piece of felt. Also it is a good idea to check for evenness by pressing the palm of your hand across the layers. Once the art of felt making has been mastered, you may want to make a feature of different thicknesses and gaps in one piece of felt.

Making the layers from slivers

If you are using slivers and you are not carding the fibres, it is relatively easy to make the layers. By pulling a small handful of fibres from the length of slivers which also spreads the fibres, it is possible to make one layer in this way. Each handful of fibres is laid down in a parallel formation onto the cotton or calico. The next layer is laid at 90° to the first, continuing in this way until the desired thickness is achieved. The same checks are necessary to make sure there are no holes or gaps.

Protecting the carded layers

Once the layers have been built up to the desired thickness, it is necessary to cover the fibres and protect them during the wet stage (see Plate 12). Gently bring the excess amount of cotton over the layers to cover all the fleece, leaving excess around the edge. With a needle and thread, sew with tacking stitches as close as possible to the fleece through the calico or

✂ **Plate 10** Making the first carded layer

✂ **Plate 11** The finished carded layers

✂ **Plate 12** Covering the carded fleece with calico

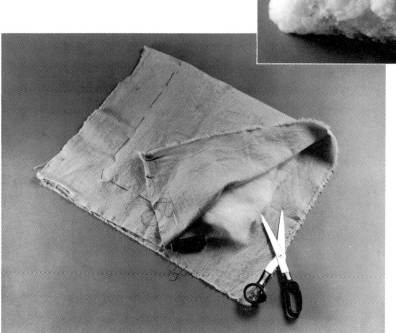

cotton. That way, all the fibres are enclosed in the cotton bag. If your intended piece of felt is quite large, additional tacking stitches diagonally across the fibres through both sides of the cotton might be a good idea. The reason for protecting the fibres is because the less the fibres move, the more even the surface of the felt, and you are less likely to get holes and faults.

HARDENING THE FIBRES

The fibres are now ready for the wet stages of felt making, known as hardening. Carefully move your protected carded fleece to the area you have decided best for this stage. It is much easier to carry it on the wooden board, this way you are not disturbing the fibres. Either keep the unmade piece of felt on the board, or carefully place in the sink, bowl or other vessel. Have the boiled water ready, or make sure the tap water is fairly hot. If you have decided to use soap or acid, have this at hand. Put on your rubber gloves and take the boiled or hot water and gently sprinkle it over the fibres evenly over the whole area. With the palms of your hands, press lightly on the fibres to push the water through the fibres (see Plate 13). Keep sprinkling with hot water until the fibres are completely saturated. Keep the fibres as flat as possible, making sure they do not crumple. If you want to use soap or acid, sprinkle a small amount over the saturated fibres. Sprinkle with a little more hot water, and with the palms of the hands gently push the water through the canvas into the fibres. With both hands flat, work evenly across the piece of felt. The fibres should begin to compress and look much flatter. When the water begins to cool, gently roll your rolling pin over the fleece to press out the water. Sprinkle with more hot water evenly over the whole area. Continue to do this for at least fifteen minutes and then check how the fleece is hardening. Undo one corner of the cotton bag and check the condition of the fibres. If the fibres are still loose, then keep patting, frequently sprinkling with hot water. When the fibres have started to link together and attach themselves to the cotton, this is a good time to remove the cotton covering. Depending on the type of fleece, this hardening process can take anything from fifteen minutes to one hour.

Using your feet

When you are happy that the fibres are reasonably compressed it is possible to use your feet instead of using hand pressure. If you use boiling water, make sure you have wellingtons on. As with your hands, use your feet with a smooth stomping motion, working evenly across the fleece (see Plate 14). Make sure the cotton doesn't lift as you bring up each foot. You should also keep checking that the fleece isn't adhering to the cotton.

When to remove the canvas

When you notice that the fibres are attaching to the cotton and are reasonably felted, it is time to remove the covering. Remove all the tacking stitches and take one corner of the cotton and gently ease the covering away from the felt. If the fibres are still very loose, keep the fibres covered. It is important to remove the covering slowly, so that you do not disturb the fibres too much. If, when the covering has been removed and there are areas that have not felted and have become loose chunks of fibre, then cut these away. This is a good time to trim the edges as well. If you have removed the covering because the fibres were attaching themselves but the fleece needs further hardening, cover loosely with the canvas and continue the hardening process.

THE MILLING STAGE

You have reached this stage when the woollen fibres have become fairly matted and you have removed the covering. Milling finishes off the hardening stage, and this is when you can see the fibres shrinking to form a firm piece of felt. As with the hardening stage, it is necessary to constantly drain away cold water and sprinkle with hot water. Use the wooden board at this stage as a surface to roll the felt on. At first, it may be a good idea to cover the felt with the cotton and then roll around the rolling pin. Sprinkle the felt with hot water, roll around the pin and with the palms of your hand, press hard and roll backwards and forwards (see Plate 15). Keep the felt tightly rolled, and every so often turn 90° and sprinkle with more hot water.

Continue to do this for as long as you feel necessary – anything from fifteen minutes to one hour. The felt will begin to be covered in ripples as the fibres shrink. The more the fibres shrink, the stronger your piece of felt will be. If you get tired, rest and return to the milling stage later. Do not cut corners by thinking you have hardened or milled it for long enough when you can see the fibres have not adhered or shrunk. Test to see if a piece of felt is well made by rubbing the felt between the thumb and index finger. If the fibres do not slip, then the felt is ready to be dried. If it is not finished, continue rolling with lots of hot water and pressure.

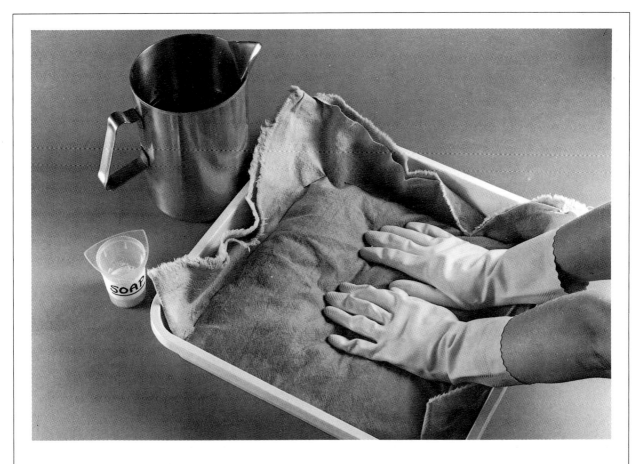

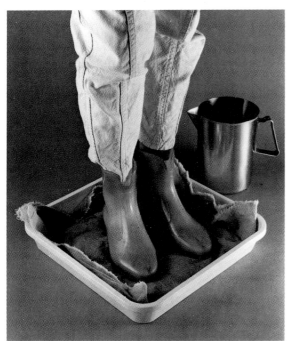

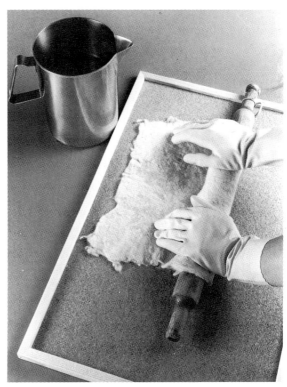

✂ **Plates 13-15** The wet stage: patting the fleece with hot water and soap; stamping on the fleece; rolling the felt after removing canvas

Plate 16 Pinning out the finished piece of felt to dry

DRYING THE FINISHED PIECE OF FELT

When you are satisfied you cannot go any further with your piece of felt, then it is ready to be dried. To remove the excess water, place the felt in a pillow case and place it in the spindryer. Alternatively, roll until no more water comes out and squeeze by hand. Now take the piece of felt and stretch and pin it onto your wooden board (see Plate 16). Put this somewhere warm to dry. It is best to dry the felt flat, so that it does not crinkle and stretch into a funny shape. Once the felt has dried, press over the entire surface area with a steam iron or wet cloth and iron. This will give the felt a smooth appearance.

Hopefully, you will have a successful piece of felt which you can keep as a sample or make into a small accessory. If you were not successful, be patient and try again – you cannot rush felt making. You may be better off using a different fleece or trying a different method (see Chapter 4).

4
ALTERNATIVE WAYS OF MAKING FELT

The previous chapter describes one way of making felt by hand, and does not include the use of machinery or other equipment. There are other ways of making felt, and you may wish to experiment. It will be useful to try different methods, as you may discover a better way of making felt for yourself, thus developing your own personal style.

THE WASHING MACHINE METHOD

Perhaps your living accommodation is totally unsuitable for the wet stages of felt making, or perhaps you find the hand-rolling method too exhausting. If so, you will want to experiment by using the washing machine. If you do so, you replace the hardening stage of the hand-rolling method in the machine, but it is still necessary to mill the felt by rolling it afterwards.

Preparation

The preparation stages are more or less the same as with the hand-rolling method. That means that you will need to wash and dry your fleece, then tease and card it. The difference is at the layer-building stage. Good preparation of the fleece is still absolutely necessary whatever the type of fleece you are using. Once you have built up the layers of carded fleece and checked for unevenness and holes, you need to secure the fibres. With a needle and thread, sew with large tacking stitches around the edge of your carded square. Then sew tacking stitches in lines 5cm (2in) apart diagonally in both directions to give a lattice effect. Be sure to sew through all the layers of fleece and do not pull the thread too tight so that you pucker the layers of fibres. Each stitch can be 10cm (4in) in length, but take care not to make holes by pulling the fibres apart. Once you have secured the fibres, you can cover the layers with canvas, calico or cotton. By doing this, you are protecting the fibres and also the washing machine. A few fibres will escape, but you can remove these by hand from the inside of the machine when you have finished.

Take the cotton covering underneath and over the top of the carded layers. Smooth out the cotton and flatten as much as possible. With a needle and thread, sew large tacking stitches through the top and bottom layer of cotton, but close to the edge of the fleece. That will encase the fleece in the cotton. When the fibres are in the washing machine, you do not want them to fall back on themselves and make uneven felt or lumps. The idea is to make the piece of felt as near to a square or rectangle as possible, therefore sew large tacking stitches through the cotton and fibres from top side to bottom diagonally in both directions. As you pull the thread through from one side to the other, take care not to pull too hard and pucker the fleece. Now roll up your parcel as tightly as possible, but keeping it as smooth as you can. When rolled tightly, bind the roll with woollen yarn to secure.

✂ **Colour Plate 3** (page 27) Making a feature of curly fleece. The felt circle has been laid out on a cane rolling mat

Placing in the washing machine

It is to your advantage to place as many pieces of felt as possible in the washing machine. One piece is not only wasteful of the cycle and load, but also several pieces help to felt each other as they tumble around. Obviously, you do not want to overload your washing machine, so place the same amount of fleece parcels equivalent to a normal washing load. Place your parcels in the drum of the machine, select a woollen wash programme, and use liquid soap. Then turn on the washing machine and wait. Before removing from the drum, make sure that the felt has been well spun.

Removing from the washing machine

Remove the parcels from the washing machine, and take them to a table to unravel. If the pieces have not unravelled themselves, then unwind them. Smooth out each parcel flat on the table, and start to unpick the stitching from the cotton covering. When you have removed all the stitches from the cotton, take one corner of the cotton and gently ease away from the piece of felt. If the covering has felted to the fleece, be very careful. Keep one hand with the palm flat on the fibres and with the other hand ease the covering away. You will need to do this on both sides to remove the covering completely. Depending on the type of fleece you have used, the piece of felt may be fairly delicate. If so, do not remove the tacking stitches from the fleece.

Milling after the washing machine

If it is necessary to keep the tacking stitches, then handle the half-made felt carefully, making sure not to stretch it. Then take your piece of felt either with the stitches still in or removed, and roll one piece of felt around the rolling pin and follow the milling process from the previous chapter (see page 24). When you are happy that the felt is shrinking and becoming firm, remove the rest of the tacking stitches. Keep rolling, using plenty of hot water and lots of hand pressure until the fibres have made a firm piece of felt. Then dry as described in Chapter 3 (page 26).

MILLING LARGE PIECES IN CANE MATS

When making large pieces of felt, the handling of the fibres can prove to be a problem. The weight of the water in the fibres means you want to lift the carded layers of fleece as little as possible or not at all. To help you, it is useful to use cane mats. A mat made from a loose warp of string and a weft of thin cane is ideal. You may know a weaver who can make you such a mat to the size you require (1m x 2m (39in x 78in) is a useful size). Alternatively, you could try weaving a mat yourself by hand. Otherwise beach mats made from natural straw or raffia can be used. Beach mats are not as durable as cane ones, therefore do not use something you will want to use again for anything other than felt making. If your mat is much larger than your smaller pieces of felt, you can always place several small pieces in the mat if this method suits you.

Prepare your fleece as described in Chapter 3, so that you are ready to build up layers of carded fleece. First lay down the cane mat, and then cover with calico or cotton cut to size. Now place the carded layers onto the cotton to cover the area of the size of the piece of felt you want to make. Make sure the fibres do not come over the edge of the calico or cane mat. Build the layers of carded fleece to the thickness you want, then cover the fleece with the cotton covering and stitch through as described in Chapter 3 (page 22). Lift your covered fleece on the cane mat to where you are going to harden the felt. The hardening process from the previous chapter can be followed, keeping the fibres on the mat.

When the cotton covering has been removed place the half-made piece of felt flat onto the cane mat. Smooth out the felt and then roll it tightly inside the cane mat. Smooth out the felt and then roll it tightly inside the cane mat. Pour on lots of water and roll the cane and felt parcel backwards and forwards. When the roll becomes loose, unravel and turn a piece of felt around 90° and re-roll tightly. Pour on more hot water and keep rolling using lots of hand pressure. Continue this procedure until you are satisfied that your felt is fully milled. When you have a strong piece of felt that is fully shrunk, you can pin it out and leave to dry.

MAKING FELT BALLS

This is a very easy and simple way to make felt, and it is an ideal method to use when making felt with children. For making felt balls, you need no equipment, just your hands, fleece, hot water and soap. Not only are the felt balls very easy to make, but they also lend themselves to many uses (see pages 56-9).

To make felt balls you need fleece that has been washed, teased and carded. Take a handful of fleece and scrunch it up in your hand to get a rough idea of how large the ball will be. Then add more fleece or take some away. It is easier to handle a small amount and then add extra fleece as your ball begins to form. To your handful of fleece add a spot of liquid soap and a splash of hot water. Then with both hands together and the fleece between the palms of your hand, gently move the hands in a circular movement with light pressure. The fleece will begin to fold into a ball. Add more fleece if you want to make the ball larger and

keep rolling the ball between the palms of your hands. Add more soap and water as you need it. Do not use too much soap as the fleece will become too slippery to handle. Continue rolling the fleece until the felt ball has become quite firm. If there are strands of fleece that have not felted in, then cut these away and continue rolling until the surface is smooth. These are so

✂ **Plates 17 & 18** Making felt balls

✂ **Plates 19-21** Making felt with rolags: using hand carders; weaving on layers of fleece; the felted rolags

easy to make and quick to produce, that you can make several in one session. This is an ideal way of using left-over fleece when making felt samples.

A SIMPLE TEXTURED PIECE OF FELT

It is easy to create a simple texture on felt with undyed fleece. If you have a fleece that is multicoloured, you can make use of the different colours. The texture is produced by making *rolags* from the carded fleece. A rolag is a roll of carded fleece that is used by a spinner to spin into the woollen yarn. To make a rolag, first card your fleece as described in Chapter 3, then roll the carded fleece lengthways into a sausage. Make about ten rolags. Now make two layers of carded fleece. Take five of your rolags and place onto the carded layers in one direction neatly next to each other (see Plate 19). Take the other five rolags and weave them between the first five rolags in the opposite direction (see Plate 20). This will give you a simple woven pattern. If your fleece is multicoloured the woven pattern will be more distinct. Secure the fleece with large tacking stitched through all the layers. Cover with a cotton covering and follow the hand-rolling method described in Chapter 3. The finished piece of felt will have an uneven texture and if your rolags were multicoloured you will end up with a piece of felt with a checked pattern. This technique can be taken further when you use dyed fleece (see page 40).

MAKING FELT ARTICLES WITH NO SEAMS

At the sampling stage it is a good idea to use your time trying different techniques that are fairly simple. A good technique to try is making a felt pocket with no seams. The obvious advantage of this method is that there is no sewing needed after the felt pocket is made. Once you are accomplished with this technique you will no doubt want to experiment with other ways of using it described further on in the book.

The first time you try this technique, make a small pocket. A sample size of 23cm (9in) square is large enough. Prepare and card the fleece and lay out the cotton covering. Place four layers of carded fleece onto the cotton covering, remembering to place alternate layers at 90° to the previous one. Now take a piece of plastic sheet (an old plastic bag with no holes will do) and then cut out a rectangle 17.5 x 23cm (7in x 9in) (see Plate 22). Place the plastic rectangle onto the carded layers leaving a margin of 2.5cm (1in) on three sides and the plastic sheet overlapping the fleece on the fourth side. Now place a further four layers

squarely on top of the first four layers and the plastic sheet. With a needle and thread sew through all the carded layers and plastic. Cover with a cotton covering and stitch through to keep the fibres in place. Now follow the hardening and milling process from Chapter 3. When you come to remove the covering check that there is a gap in the middle of the felt where the plastic is. If the opening has become felted and closed then cut through the fibres with a pair of scissors. Just before you finish milling the felt remove the plastic. The edges should be felted together leaving the centre open to be used as a pocket. Chapter 8 shows further ideas using this technique.

MAKING FELT IN THE SHAPE OF THE FINISHED ARTICLE

One of the advantages of designing with fibres and making felt is that you are not restricted to rectangles or squares. Usually it is most convenient to make felt in regular shapes and so far all samples described for making felt use the square format. As you develop your felt making you may well want to produce shapes that are irregular to suit the shape of the finished article. This is relatively easy to do whether you are using prepared fleece slivers or unprepared fleece. Once you have produced rectangular and circular pieces of felt you will be able to produce more or less any shape you want.

Using unprepared fleece
Follow all the preparation stages up to the carding of the fleece. You may find it easier to card several laps of fleece. That way when you come to organise the layers all your fleece will be carded and then you can concentrate on forming the shape. Therefore either hand card or drum card several layers of fleece and place on one side. Now take a piece of cotton bigger than the size of your intended shape. Smooth out the calico and if it has been used before remove any fibres that have been left behind. If the cotton is very crumpled iron it smooth. To make a circular piece of felt it helps to draw a circle on to the cotton covering. Remember the felt will shrink, therefore draw your circle 5cm (2in) larger than the size you want your piece of felt to be. Draw the circle in pencil or tailor's chalk.

To make a circle from carded fleece
Using the chalk circle as your guide line, take one carded lap of fleece and place it in the centre of the circle (see Plate 25). Now take the other carded laps and place around the first making sure they all face in the same direction and there are no gaps. Some of the fleece will overlap the drawn circle so take a pair of

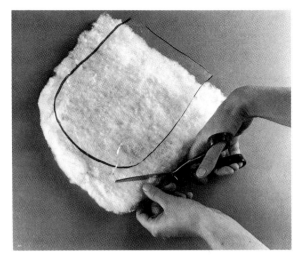

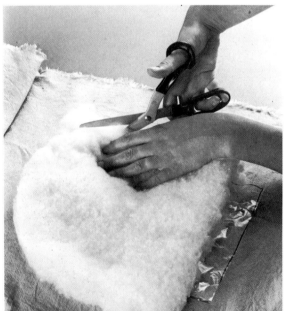

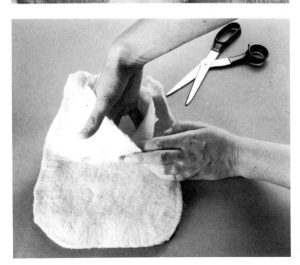

scissors and trim away the fleece using your drawn circle as a guideline. This will leave you with one layer of fleece in a neat circle.

For the next layer follow the same procedure but remember to place your fibres at 90° to the first layer. Trim the overlapping fleece using the first layer as your guideline. Continue to build the layers until you have reached the desired thickness. Check for holes and gaps and fill the gaps with blobs of carded fleece.

If you are using a drum carder, depending on the size of your circle, you may find you can make two layers from one carded lap. Do not make your circle too large when trying this for the first time; 23cm (9in) in diameter will be large enough for a sample.

Making a circle from prepared fleece slivers

This fleece will not need so much preparation. Most important it will not need to be carded and is therefore relatively easy to use. Start by drawing a circle onto your cotton covering. This guideline is essential. Now take the fleece slivers in one hand. Start at the bottom of the circle and pull a small amount of fibres from the length of sliver and place onto the cotton covering. Work from the bottom of the circle and then from left to right, leaving small handfuls of fleece as you go. Try to overlap each deposit of fibres to avoid gaps. Trim away any fibres that overlap the drawn circle. Start the next layer placing the fibres at 90° to the first layer. Continue to build the layers until you reach the desired thickness. It is important when using slivers of fleece not to pull out large clumps of fleece so that you produce lumpy layers. If you do this your finished piece of felt will be lumpy and prone to holes.

To protect the fleece circle

Having built up the layers of fleece to produce your felt circle you will now need to protect it for the hardening stage. Take your cotton covering and fold it over the fleece circle or take another covering and place it over the circle. Pin around the edge of the circle through both cotton coverings. With large tacking stitches stitch through the cotton coverings as close as possible to the fleece circle. Handle carefully so as not to disturb the fibres – to help protect the fibres you will need to sew through all the layers of cotton and fleece. Start from the centre of the circle and with large tacking stitches sew through all the layers working in a spiral formation from the centre outwards. Make sure not to pull the thread too tight so

✄ **Plates 22-24** Making a seamless pocket: cutting the fleece around the pattern; the finished pocket

✂ **Plates 25-27** Making felt in the shape of a circle: cutting the first layer; sewing the fleece into calico; the finished circle

that you do not disturb the fibres or pucker the covering. Keep the fleece parcel as smooth as possible and carefully carry it to the place set aside for the wet stage. Now follow the steps for hardening either from Chapter 3 or the washing-machine process. If you choose to place it in the washing machine roll it tightly first and bind with woollen yarn.

MAKING A FEATURE OF CURLY FLEECE

Fleece is incredibly tactile and therefore so is felt. When it comes to choosing fleece you will be aware of the variety that is available. It is worth experimenting with the longer curly fleeces as you can make some very interesting designs with it (see Fibre Chart in Chapter 2). The best way to make a feature of the curly fleece is to use it on the edges of your piece of felt. An interesting example of this is to make a felt circle with curly fleece edges (see Colour Plate 3). Then experiment by using this detail on pockets or bags and maybe even waistcoats.

Making a curly fleece edge on a circle

Follow the instructions for making a felt circle. Stop when you have made half the layers you need. This will be the centre of your piece of felt. Now take your curly fleece. The staple length may be about 15cm (6in). If the base of your curly fleece staple is very tangled trim this away with scissors. Take several handfuls of curly fleece and tease each handful slightly, just to untangle and separate the fibres to make the hardening easier. Try to use fleece that is not dirty so that you do not need to wash it (this would tangle the long fibres). Place a handful of fleece inside the circle with the end of the staple 10cm (4in) inside and the curly tips radiating outside the circle. Place all the way around the fleece circle in this way to produce a fringe. Then continue with the top layers of carded fleece. Trim the carded fleece to make a neat circle leaving the curly fleece fringe exposed but trapped between the layers.

This now has to be covered with the cotton covering to protect it. Place the cotton covering over the fleece making sure not to ruffle the fringe. You will need to sew two circles of stitching to secure the fibres. First of all sew through both layers of cotton close to the edge of the carded fleece. Then sew a second line close to the tips of the curly fleece. For added protection sew through the cotton covering and the fleece circle and the spiral formation described previously. Do not place in the washing machine to harden as this will felt the fringe. This must be hardened by the hand-rolling method. At the hardening stage work only on the fleece circle outlined with stitching. When rolling the felt take care not to tangle the fringe, but pull the fibres straight every so often as you turn the felt.

Once felted it may be necessary to tease the fringe to open out the fibres where they have become slightly felted. To make a feature of the curly fringe you may want to brush it. Take a stiff brush and gently brush the fibres with stroking movements at the base where they are felted in. Make sure you do not tug the fibres otherwise they may pull out.

DISCOVERING OTHER METHODS OF MAKING FELT

It is well worth listening to other felt makers and learning their method of making felt. The methods described in this book are to help you achieve a smooth uniform piece of felt.

Perhaps you would like to try one very interesting method that a lady from New Zealand described to me which sounds fascinating. The method involves taking the carded fleece protected in a covering. This is then plunged into cold water and then hot water and is finished off by being beaten against a tree. The final piece of felt is evidently very attractive and strong.

By now you will have some felt samples in natural fleece and have found the best way and place for making your felt. If you want to expand your felt making it is worth using coloured fleece to produce even more exciting samples. I hope Chapter 5 on exploring colour will encourage you to take your felt making even further.

ℋ **Colour Plate 4** A batch of dyed fleece

5
EXPLORING COLOUR

When the basic principles of making felt have been understood and tried using natural coloured fleeces, it is exciting to progress to coloured fleece. Natural coloured fleeces have lovely qualities and colours of their own, but using colour opens up a whole new area of felt making. Your own personal style will develop because you are wholly in control of your fabric from dyeing the colours to making the felt, and eventually making finished products.

Using coloured fleece does not mean that felt making becomes more complicated. In fact, you may find you become inspired by colour and this helps you when designing. There are three choices you have when using coloured fleece. You can either buy fleece that is already dyed, or you can dye the fleece yourself using natural dyes or chemical dyes.

BUYING DYED FLEECE

Maybe you do not have time to dye your own fleece and would rather spend more time designing and making your felt. If this is the case, then it is possible to buy fleece already dyed. Most spinning suppliers can offer you a range of dyed fleece in small or large amounts. Send for samples of their colour range. You may have to pay for samples but they are well worth having as they may become a source of reference for colour and texture later. When you ask for samples, be sure to ask for the count of the fleece to make sure you order the best quality for felt making. Very often dyed fleece may be a mixture blend of different fleeces. This doesn't matter but you want a blend with a high count of around 60. Remember the higher the count, the easier it is to felt. If you buy dyed fleece it will either be in slivers or a carded vat. Either is suitable to use for felt making. If the fibre in the sliver is long, you can cut it to a shorter length. Remember when sampling with dyed fleece you will not need to buy large amounts. It may be better to buy several colours and smaller amounts. 100g (4oz) is a good amount to start with. It helps to keep the amount to round figures – this assists with any mathematics that may be involved. When you know what colours you prefer to use for a specific design, you can order more in quantity.

Buying dyed fleece is obviously going to be more expensive than buying natural fleece, but you are saving time not having to dye it yourself or prepare the fleece. If you do not have facilities for dyeing, at least you are not restricted to having to use only natural coloured fleece. You will be inspired by colour.

DYEING YOUR OWN FLEECE

Dyeing fleece is an art in itself. It is a pleasure to take a natural-coloured fleece and turn it into a palette of rainbow colours. Dyeing is a very messy occupation, best done in a garage or shed or simply the garden. Do not be put off, you can always dye small amounts which makes dyeing much easier.

Which dyes to use

You have the option of using chemical dyes or natural dyes. Both types offer a wide range of hues and tones, and it is often down to personal preference. The methods of dyeing are fairly different as are the finished results. If you have not done any dyeing before, it is well worth reading a good book on the subject before you buy your dyes and equipment. Consult your library or bookshop. Whether you are dyeing cloth, yarn or fleece, the principles are much the same.

There are many dye companies that sell dyes but not all of them will supply you with small quantities. You may find it is far cheaper to buy large amounts and then split the quantity with other people. It isn't just a case of buying the dyes, you will also need to buy other chemicals that act as a catalyst in the dyeing procedure. When purchasing dyes and chemicals, you must make sure you are buying the correct type for woollen fibres. Do check with your supplier that you are being offered the correct type and ask about colour and light fastness. You will not want the colour to fade in the light or disappear when at the wet stage of felt making or washing. Also, check that the dyeing procedure does not include boiling for any length of time. This may be compensated for by adding more chemicals to assist with the penetration of the dye into the fleece.

Chemical dyes

Chemical dyes are relatively easy to purchase and use. They can be bought in powder or liquid form and should come with their own dye recipe of what chemicals you will need and what quantities. Remember you can always dye your fleece a darker shade, but you cannot make it any lighter. When using chemical dyes, it is worth starting with a weaker solution of dye and then add more colour if necessary. Before dyeing a large amount of fleece, always test the colour first on a small sample. This will save time in the long run. By buying a limited range of colours in different concentrations, you will be able to achieve lots of shades. Therefore it is not necessary to buy a wide range. It is fun to experiment by mixing your own colours. Depending on how sophisticated the dyes are, they may well only come in a limited range, so you will have to mix your own recipes. By mixing your coloured fleece by blending whilst carding it will not matter if you do not dye many colours (see Blending colours, page 41).

Natural dyes

If you choose to use natural dyes you can make the procedure complicated or as easy as you like. By buying a book on natural dyes, this will give you an idea of what is involved. It is possible to collect the natural plants yourself or purchase them dried from a supplier. There are many chemicals that are needed for natural dyeing depending on what plant you are using. Natural dyes are preferred by some people for the beautiful range of soft hues that can be achieved. It is worth taking into consideration that the dyes will vary more than chemical dyes depending on the quality of the plants you are using. Each batch of materials may vary, giving a slightly different shade. Therefore it is more difficult to achieve the same colour again. If you decide to use natural dyes, you will undoubtedly find the process both rewarding and interesting.

WHAT COLOURS TO DYE

Depending on the dyes you have chosen to use, you may have a large range of colours to choose from or a limited range. It will be the same if you are buying dyed fleece. You will probably find it is easier to start with five colours to experiment with. If you only want to use two or three different shades, then you will still achieve an interesting effect. When deciding what colours to choose, it is best to keep to colours of the same tone. That is, keep to pastel or bright shades. Then in the range of shades you decide upon, choose good contrasting colours.

Bright colours

If you decide you want to use bright colours and you want to use five different shades, a good choice would be black (as your dark contrast), a deep strong blue (cobalt), a good strong red (poppy red), a deep yellow (sunflower), and a strong pink (fuchsia pink). If you are dyeing your own fleece, it is a good idea to keep some fleece undyed to blend with your colours.

Pastels

Perhaps you prefer pastel colours and more subtle tones, but again it is a good idea to choose colours that contrast. Black would be too harsh to mix with pastel colours, so choose either a mid-grey or soft brown as your dark contrast. Then a pale blue, a soft pink, peach rather than yellow and a pale green. Again, keep some fleece undyed to mix with your colours.

DYEING THE FLEECE

Whether you use chemical dyes or natural dyes, there is a certain amount of basic equipment you will need and a few points worth taking note of.

Equipment

Domestic cooker or gas rings – for heating water
Large pots and pans – made from enamel or stainless steel
Buckets and bowls – plastic or stainless steel
Scales – for weighing fleece and dyes
    (this can be avoided by making a dye concentrate and then measuring a spoonful of liquid dye)
Glass jars – for mixing dyes
Spoons   – for measuring, mixing and stirring
Muslin   – for placing the fleece in when dyeing
Storage jars – for keeping the dyes and chemicals in. Airtight and made of glass
Rubber gloves – to protect and keep your hands clean
Apron – to protect your clothes from splashing
Wellingtons – to guard your feet from hot water and dye
Spindryer – optional but does help to remove excess water and dye from fleece.

✂ **Plate 28** Dyeing equipment

✂ **Colour Plate 6** Mixing coloured fleece in the hand carders

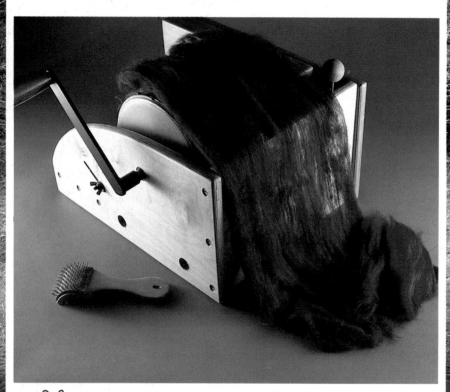

✂**Colour Plate 7** One layer of carded fleece carded on the drum carder

✂ **Colour Plate 5** (large picture) Carded fleece using four different colours

Where to dye

Now you can see what equipment is involved, decide where to do your dyeing. It is worth doing it well away from anything you do not want to be damaged. Read the directions carefully for the dyes you have chosen, and make sure you have everything you need at hand.

Points worth noting

Before you dye your fleece, make sure it is clean and dry. If it needs washing, follow instructions in Chapter 3. You will need to weigh your fleece to ensure the correct ratio of dye for the quantity of fleece. Therefore the fleece must be dry when you weigh it. Always use a vessel for dyeing that allows plenty of room for the fleece to move around in the water. If you do not allow for much movement the fleece may well dye unevenly (this can also be used as a feature). Handle the fleece very carefully to avoid tangles. Therefore it is a good idea to tie your fleece loosely in a muslin bag allowing plenty of room for movement whilst in the dye bath. This will enable you to remove the fleece much more easily from the water than if it was floating unprotected.

It is a good idea to saturate the fleece in hot water before dyeing as this helps the fleece to take up the dye more evenly. Make sure the centre of the fleece bundle gets saturated with hot water. If the dye you are using is in powder form make sure that it is well diluted and well dispersed in the water. Once the fleece is in the dye vessel, move around gently with a spoon. During the dyeing process, move the fleece around quite frequently and this will dye it more evenly. Again, make sure the centre of the bundle gets saturated with dye.

If a dye recipe says boil for one hour, do not keep the fleece in boiling water for this length of time. If you do, there is a fair chance that your fleece will become matted and felt during the dyeing process. The best thing to do is to raise the temperature to boiling and then turn the heat down or off and add more chemicals if necessary.

Some dyes are far stronger than others, and some fleeces take up the dye better than others. If you do decide to add more dye or chemicals, you should remove the fleece from the water to guarantee even distribution. Remove the fleece and add the dye, stirring in well and then return the fleece.

Dye the fleece for the recommended amount of time on the dye instructions. If the fleece has absorbed the dye well, you will be left with coloured fleece and the water will be pale in colour. Test the fleece before removing from the dye vessel by running a handful under hot water to remove excess dye. If the fleece is a good strong colour, and no more dye is coming out, the fleece is ready.

When you have finished dyeing, remove the fleece in the muslin bag and place into a bucket or sink of hot water to rinse. Keep rinsing in hot water until no more dye is running out from the fleece. Place in warm water, then tepid and then finally cold water. To remove excess water, place the fleece in its muslin bag in a spindryer. It is important to rinse your fleece well until the colour doesn't run any more, because you do not want it to run when you are making your felt. If you are making felt from many different coloured fleeces, you may end up with a dirty piece of felt if your colours run.

To dry the fleece, place it somewhere airy and warm. Either hang on the washing line in the muslin bag or open out and place in an airing cupboard. Once the fleece is dry you are ready for the preparation stages of felt making. You will probably find the fleece needs teasing well after dyeing.

HOW TO USE YOUR DYED FLEECE

There are several ways you can make felt with dyed fleece. If you have just started making felt, or have not used coloured fleece before, it is worth experimenting and trying all the techniques listed here. Remember when you are making samples of felt, it makes sense to harden several pieces at one time to save time and energy.

Layers of Colours

The simplest way to make use of your coloured fleece is to make different coloured layers. The advantage of making felt in coloured layers is that you can make a feature of the edges. First of all, decide how thick you want your piece of felt to be, and then decide how many layers. If you decide to make five layers, then use either three or five colours of fleece. To make the best feature of the edges, use good contrasting colours.

For example (see Plate 5), if you choose to use five colours, start with your first layer of carded fleece in red, the second in yellow, third in black, the fourth in pink and the final and fifth layer in blue. Each time you card a new colour, make sure you have removed all the coloured fleece from the previous carding. Gradually build up your sandwich of coloured carded fleece. Make sure to keep each layer the same thickness and remember to alternate each layer at 90° to the previous one.

If you decide you only want to use three colours, but you want five layers for the right thickness, then make the first, middle and last layer the same colour, and make the second and fourth layer each different colours, eg red, blue, red, yellow, red.

If you are using coloured fleece tops or slivers that do not need carding, then follow the laying-out instructions in Chapter 3 (page 22). Do remember to keep the layers even and to the same thickness. Once you have prepared the carded layers, you can continue with one of the hardening stages as described on page 24 or 28. Your finished piece of multicoloured layered felt will be interesting in two ways. Not only will you have a multicoloured edge when you cut through the felt, but also it will be a different colour on each side. During the hardening and milling stages, the colours on the second and fourth layer will blend with the outside layers. Therefore where you have red next to yellow, the red will appear slightly orange; where the blue is next to the strong pink, it will appear slightly purple. This effect can be enhanced by using thinner layers.

The finished piece of felt will need to be trimmed around the edges to show off the multicoloured edge. Chapter 6 will give you more ideas for using multicoloured layered felt.

Blending colours when carding

By blending colours at the carding stage, you will appreciate using dyed fleece even more. Blending your different coloured fleece is like mixing paints. Whether you choose to blend two or more colours together, the effect will be interesting and rewarding. The technique is very simple as the colours are mixed in the carders. If your fleece comes in sliver form, you will need to card it to benefit from the finished effect of blending colours. Cut it to 2in (5cm) lengths if the staple is very long. When blending colours in the carders, you have the choice of the finished effect. Either you can blend them really well to produce a new smooth colour, or you can blend them slightly to produce a more speckled effect.

Start off by deciding how many colours you want to mix. If you want to blend two colours, choose two strong contrasting colours, for example green and blue (see Colour Plate 6). Card each colour separately and thoroughly. If you are using hand carders, first take the red and place onto the carder and make a few movements with the carders. Now take the blue fleece and place onto the carder and continue to card the two colours together. Gradually the two colours will mix together. Keep carding until the colours are blended to your liking. If you want the two colours very well blended, then remove the fleece from the carders and re-card the fleece again. Continue carding until you are happy with the effect. If you want to mix three colours, then place all these colours on the carders and keep carding until they are well blended. Card enough fleece in this way until you

have enough carded fleece to make a felt sample.

If you are using a drum carder, you can achieve a different effect. Decide on the colours you want to blend. Place one colour through the drum carder and then the next colour and then the third. Remove the carded lap and place through the drum carder again. This will produce a very well-blended mix of coloured fleece.

Alternatively, you could place the first colour through the drum carder and with the second and third carder, just catch the fibres onto the drum as you rotate it. Place the fibres in small amounts evenly across the teeth. Do not put on big clumps of fleece as these will catch in the carders. Turn the handle of the drum carder a few times and this will give you a fairly speckled layer of carded fleece for a felt sample (see Colour Plate 7).

Effects achieved by blending colours

When you start blending your coloured fleece, you will realise how, from a limited range of colours, you can produce a variety of effects. If you are mixing blue and yellow together when it is well blended you will be able to produce a felt that appears green. If you have chosen to use bright colours but you want them to appear softer, it is possible to dilute them by blending them with the natural coloured fleece. A bright pink can be made paler by adding a lot of natural coloured fleece. If a darker shade of red is wanted, then blend your red with a small amount of black. Do not just keep to colours that you know mix well together. If you mix your red with a small amount of bright pink, this can have a stunning effect. At the same time though, be careful not to blend colours that end up looking dirty, which can happen if you blend colours that are tonally very similar.

If you are unsure how well colours will blend together and what the finished effect will be then try a sample first. Take tiny amounts of fleece, just a pinch of different colours, and then tease them together so they are well mixed. Then follow the instructions for making felt balls in your hand in Chapter 4, and this will give you a fairly good idea of how the finished piece of felt will look.

A very interesting effect that can be produced is a double-sided piece of felt, made to be one colour on one side and different on the other side. Try this interesting experiment: Start with the first layer in blue and gradually through the layers add more yellow and finish with the last layer in yellow. This will not only give you a double-faced piece of felt but also, when you cut through the layers, the felt will gradually change from blue to green to yellow.

MIXING DIFFERENT TYPES OF FLEECE

It isn't only mixing colours that can change the look of your felt. You can also mix different types of fleece for an interesting texture. Keep to the high count soft fibre fleeces for the base of your felt, and then add small amounts of coarser or different textured fleeces (see Fibre Chart in Chapter 2).

Exotic fleeces

Exotic fleeces are interesting to use, but do cost considerably more. Therefore it is a good idea to blend them with your basic fleece. Some of the long fleeces can be difficult to handle because they are slippery, but blended with your basic fleece they can have a luxurious effect.

Alpaca and mohair fibres have a very long staple length. Rather than cut the staple shorter, keep the length and blend them with your basic fleece. Blend them well at the carding stage and once the piece of felt has been made and dried, you can retain the length of the fibre by brushing the felt. This gives a very interesting texture and produces a hairy, silky felt. If you have used a blend of mixed coloured fibres, brushing will bring out the different colours.

If you prefer a coarser felt this can be achieved by blending your basis fleece with a fleece of a lower count and different texture. Coarse fleeces are generally difficult to felt but if you mix them with your basic fleece, you will find the hardening stage much easier. The finished piece of felt will be interesting because the coarse fibres will be visible in your piece of felt and have a slightly spiky appearance.

Long curly fleeces

Long curly fleeces look very attractive before they are made into felt. Chapter 4 describes how to make a feature of curly fleece on the surface. As you are carding the layers for a piece of felt, gradually add in more curly fleece so that the top layer is completely curly fleece. Do not cut the length of the staple. After the hardening and milling stage, a piece of felt made from long curly fleece will have a streaky effect. This is produced from the natural texture of the long fibre. If you are using coloured long curly fibres that have been blended, you will end up with wisps of colour on the surface of the felt.

Silk fibres

A really lovely fibre to add to your felt is silk. Silk fibre can be bought in sliver form and looks as luxurious as it feels. By blending silk fibre to your basic fleece you can produce a very beautiful felt, particularly when seen in the light. Silk fibre can be dyed with your fleece and takes colour very well. Generally silk fibres are fairly long in length. When blending the silk with your fleece, it is a good idea to cut the fibre to 5cm (2in) lengths; this will make it easier to card with the fleece. If you want to blend silk with a longer fleece, it will not be necessary to cut it but comb it instead with your hand carders, as this will separate the fibres. Silk will not felt into the fleece if it is left in big clumps, and this is a waste of the silk. When carding the layers, there is no point adding silk into the middle layers. Use it only on the outside layers where it will be seen. To make a feature of the silk, use contrasting colours of fleece and silk. For example, black fleece with fuchsia pink silk looks very attractive. To make this luxurious felt you only need a little silk as it goes quite a long way, so use it sparingly on the surface.

When drum carding, place the silk on the drum. Gently pull the silk across the spikes and a small amount will catch onto the teeth. Place onto the hand carders in a similar way. For a speckled effect cut the silk into 1cm (0.3in) lengths and place onto the carded fleece whilst on the carders. Then gently make a couple of movements with the carders. This will mix the silk just enough with the fleece. Silk can be used for highlighting patterns in felt and placed directly onto the surface of your carded layers.

This chapter should have broadened your horizons and you will now find you have many options to choose from. Therefore it is a good idea to try them all in small sample-size pieces of felt. You can use these samples later to make into small gifts or alternatively keep for reference. Due to the variety of effects you can achieve it will be worth making a note of what fibres you used and what dyes you used, also how many layers and what ratio of blended fibres and colours. Kept as a source of reference, this will help you when you want to make a larger piece. If you want to repeat a particular colour that you liked, it is helpful to have something to refer to, as this will save time. Do not throw away any discarded pieces of fleece, even if the colours are blended. All oddments are useful to keep. Either you can make a multicoloured piece of felt or lots of felt balls.

It is likely that using coloured fleece has inspired you to produce your own designs. Chapter 6 takes this a stage further with ideas of how to decorate the surface of your felt. Make sure you have lots of coloured fleece to try out other techniques of making patterns and textures.

6
MAKING
PATTERNED FELT

Once you have tried making felt with coloured
fleece and mixing your fibres, you will no doubt
want to produce a patterned felt. The scope
for designing patterns in felt is really
unlimited, and the design you choose will be
your own individual one. You do not need
sophisticated training in design to make a
pattern. This chapter gives a variety of ideas
on how to pattern your felt, but you will no
doubt soon have lots of your own.

It is possible to make your pattern as simple or as complicated as you like. Mixing the colours at the carding stage makes a good base for your pattern. The exciting thing about making felt is that you can make a pattern on both sides of the felt or each side can have a different design. Obviously if you decide to make a complicated design then more care is necessary at the preliminary stages.

Making the pattern on a piece of felt is done at the final stage of making the layers. When experimenting it is a good idea to have lots of layers of carded fleece made up into sample-size 23cm (9in) pieces, that are ready to be decorated. When you know what you want you can then make larger pieces or pieces of felt made in the shape of the finished article.

After placing the final carded layer of fleece, decide how large you want the pattern to be. If you are making small pieces of felt you will probably want your pattern to be small or make one large motif. When making larger pieces you may well want the pattern to be bigger. The pattern you decide to make may be a design that can be repeated over a large area similar to a pattern on printed fabric or you may prefer an unrepeated pattern. If you are sampling a design that is intended to be a distinctive motif that could be placed on a pocket of a jacket or the front of a bag, then it helps to keep your sample pattern to the size of the finished article.

There are many ways you can decorate your felt, and it is well worth trying all of them. The simplest way is to use woollen yarn and tufts of coloured fleece or you could use silk or fancy synthetic yarns. An interesting way is to combine the fleece with other materials such as net or lace to produce pattern and texture or make a lacy square from yarn by knitting and then placing onto the carded fleece. To make more sophisticated patterns of defined shapes it is possible to cut shapes from half-made felt. An interesting but rather difficult thing to do is to add woven fabric like silk or wool. This does need a lot of patience and may take a lot of sampling to find the right materials.

WHICH SIDE TO PLACE THE PATTERN

The first thing you need to decide is which side of the felt you want to make the pattern. The most natural place would be to put the pattern on the top side. Make the surface to be decorated as smooth as possible, having already checked there are no lumps or holes in the carded layers. Then you can decorate straight onto the top carded layer.

If you want to decorate the bottom layer and make your top layer a blend of colours carded together,

then start with the blended carded layer first and treat your bottom layer as the top layer. It is always easier to decorate the top layer rather than the bottom layer. Of course, you may want the felt to be decorated on both sides, if so you will then be decorating the top and bottom layers. To make this simple for yourself, it is best to decorate the top layer of carded fleece and then very carefully turn your carded layers and design over, placing the design at the bottom. Then you can decorate the other side. This will produce a double-sided patterned piece of felt. When the pattern is being placed onto the carded fleece it is obviously very delicate. Therefore before turning over the carded layers you will need to secure the top pattern. This can be done by stitching through the pattern into the top layer of carded fleece. Once the pattern has been placed on one side or both sides of the carded layers, it is even more essential to take care when covering with the cotton covering. The covering is important because you do not want to disturb your carefully placed pattern. When you reach the hardening stage it is best to harden by hand rather than foot. Milling can only be carried out once you are sure the pattern has adhered to the fleece and it is well felted in.

It helps before you start making your patterned felt to have all the materials and equipment you will need close to hand. Therefore make sure you have a needle and thread, scissors, enough cotton coverings for all your samples and plenty of dyed fleece that has already been well carded and colours blended where necessary. A good flat surface to work on also helps, then it is possible to lay out all the carded fleece into layers for your samples. Most important is to gather all the materials and yarns you are going to use to decorate the felt. If you knit you will probably have a bag full of yarns left over from knitting garments. These oddments will be very useful. If you do not have any yarns you will need to buy some specially for felt making. If you do a lot of dressmaking or sewing you may well have a box of material remnants, some of which may be suitable for combining with fleece. Not all fabrics or all yarns will felt in, so be prepared for failures when experimenting. This is why it is always a good idea to sample first to save time in the long run. Now all you need to do is to follow the directions and make your own patterned felt.

DECORATING WITH YARN

If you can spin wool this will be to your advantage because you can spin yarn from the same fleece that you have carded for the layers. If you do not spin, then it doesn't matter because there are lots of yarns you can buy that are hand spun or appear to be hand spun. When looking for yarn to decorate felt with, choose a yarn that is soft, not harsh. The yarn has to be a similar texture to your fleece for it to blend with the fleece. Only buy a harsh yarn if you are making felt from a fleece which is coarse. Woollen yarn made from natural fibres will blend in better with the fleece rather than a synthetic, although a mixture of wool and synthetic will probably work fairly well.

Once you have chosen the colours of your fleece, choose yarns that complement these colours. To make a pattern with yarns that will stand out well use a yarn of good colour contrast. The yarns you decide to use can be thick or thin, fluffy or smooth. Indeed, it is interesting to produce a design made from both types of yarn. It will help to pay a visit to a good wool shop or send for samples from yarn specialists.

Mohair is particularly good to use. The contrast of smooth fleece and the texture of fluffy mohair looks very good. Mohair blends quite well with fleece because the fibres spread out and catch into the fleece during the hardening process. There are some lovely mohair yarns available in plain colours or interesting colour mixtures, so a variety of mohair is a good

choice. Other luxurious yarns made from alpaca or camel blend well with fleece. Yarn made from these can be bought fairly fine and makes a good contrast to fluffy mohair.

Do not just select smooth or regular woollen yarns because some of the textured yarns look very interesting when felted into the fleece. The choice of fancy yarns is staggering. Yarns that are spun and varying in thickness along the strand are good fun to use as are the random-dyed yarns and yarns which have fibres every so often along the yarn. A feature can be made of the tufts.

Method

Place the prepared carded layers onto a piece of calico or cotton large enough to cover the whole piece on both sides. To decorate one side, decorate the top surface. See Fig 6 for ideas on where to place yarns and decide how you want to make a pattern. Then choose yarns in colours that work well with the fleece

Fig 6 Decorating the fleece with yarn: stripes; grid formation; diamond checks; circular formation; small bows; and small tassles

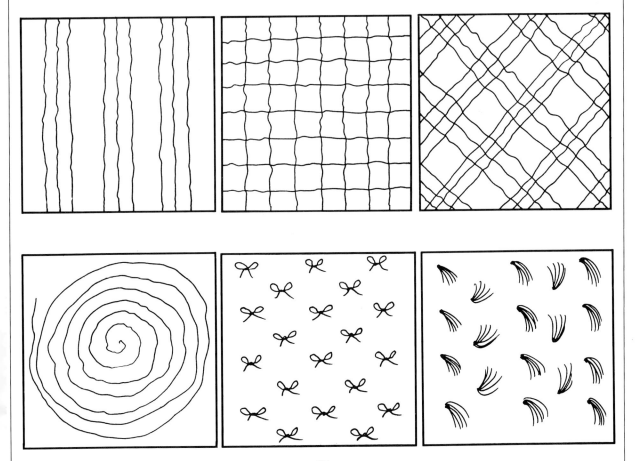

🪡 **Colour Plate 8** A piece of double-sided patterned felt (unmade)

background and try to combine a smooth yarn with fancy yarn. Alternatively, make one sample using smooth yarn and another using fluffy yarn.

Stripes

The easiest pattern to make is a striped one. Just because it is easy, it doesn't mean it can't look interesting. Imagine a black background of fleece with flecks of fuchsia pink silk fibre. To this add a fluffy mohair yarn in turquoise and a smooth yarn in bright purple. Make the stripes equal distances apart of alternate turquoise and then purple yarn. The colours and textures of the yarns will make an interesting contrast to the black and fuchsia background.

When placing the yarn onto the fleece pull a length of yarn across the carded fleece and cut the yarn to the width of your square of fleece. Continue cutting lengths of yarn until you have covered the fleece with stripes. Do not pull the yarn too tight otherwise when you cut the yarn it will shrink back and will not be long enough to stretch across the fleece.

The yarn can also be placed diagonally across the surface of the carded fleece. A combination of three colours and textures will add interest to this stripey

formation, eg a green and blue blended fleece background covered with stripes of bright pink fluffy mohair, a thin smooth yellow yarn, and a random-dyed yarn of all those colours. There are so many colour combinations you can try.

Lattice design

Once you have experimented with stripes, the next pattern to naturally try is checks or a lattice pattern. To do this you are making stripes with yarn horizontally and vertically across the carded fleece. There are several ways you can do this. The most obvious way is to place your wool in horizontal stripes first and then place the vertical stripes over the top of these. To make this more interesting, try weaving your second placement of yarn through the yarn you placed on the fleece first. During the hardening process, the inter-woven yarn will interlock. If you have chosen contrast-ing colours the effect will be more exciting.

As an alternative to this you could lay one horizontal stripe and then a vertical stripe continually across the carded fleece. This would give you a woven effect but in a different formation where the yarns overlap. By placing the yarns at irregular intervals rather than equal distances each time, you will produce a less regimental stripey pattern.

Securing the pattern

The stripes of yarn will move around at the hardening stage. This will soften the line of the yarn as it will shrink at a different rate to the fleece. If you want to keep the pattern as straight as possible, you will need to secure the yarn. With a needle and thread tack large stitches loosely around the yarn and into the top layer of fleece. Do not pull the thread too tight. If your yarns overlap, just a stitch at the intersection will hold them in place.

Placing the yarn in cut lengths

By cutting the yarn into short lengths you can produce lots of different designs. Squiggles or shapes can be made by cutting the yarn into 12.5cm (5in) lengths and this pattern looks especially good if you use lots of different coloured yarns. This idea could be combined with a stripe. Try making a spiral from a continuous length of yarn covering the whole surface of the fleece. As an alternative, smaller lengths of yarn could be used to make lots of smaller spirals. A turquoise background of fleece with small spirals of multicoloured random-dyed yarn of contrasting pink, blues and yellows would make an interesting combination.

It is worthwhile taking the time to tie the yarn into loose knots and bows and placing these onto the fleece to make a pattern. With very soft yarns, try making a small pom-pon with a small amount of yarn. This will make a pretty star or daisy shape in your felt. If you have a yarn with tufts of mohair in, you can use the tufts to make irregular spots.

To make a very textured piece of felt, try decorating the last two layers of fleece with yarns. If you use a thick yarn on the penultimate layer and make the last layer of fleece fairly thin, then the yarn will show through. By taking a good handful of 12cm (5in) lengths of a mixture of yarns lying parallel to each other and then snip a tiny amount of yarn, you will produce a speckled design. This is a very quick way to make a pattern on the felt and looks interesting mixed with stripes of yarn or larger motifs.

Preparing the pattern for hardening

Make sure you have secured the pattern well with loose tacking stitches. Then cover over with the cotton covering and stitch through the covering around the edge of the fleece to encase the carded fleece square in the cotton. Begin by sprinkling with hot water and a little soap and then very gently with flat hands pat the fleece. This will push the hot water

Colour Plate 9 Decorating the carded fleece with silk thread and mohair

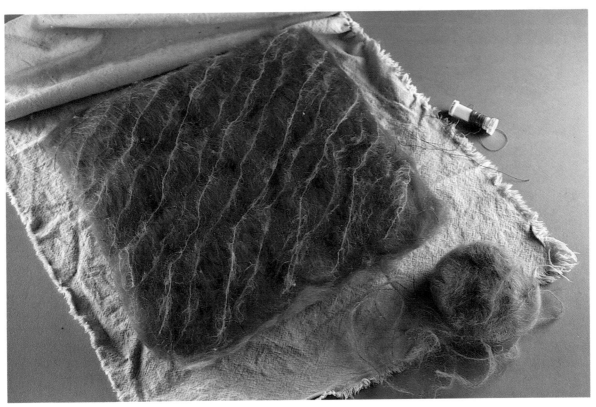

and soap through the layers. Do not stamp on the fleece until it is quite flat. Check to make sure the yarn isn't attaching itself to the cotton covering. If it is, then carefully remove the covering and stitch the yarn into the fleece with loose tacking stitches. This will have to be done very carefully so that the carded layers of fleece are not disturbed. Cover over again and continue patting and stamping. If you are hardening several pieces at once, rotate them by moving the top one to the bottom every so often. At the rolling stage you should be able to see that the yarn has started to felt in quite well. If after rolling, the yarn has only felted in to some areas, it will be better to cut away any loose yarn as after a while it will not felt in at all. Placing a thin layer of fleece over the yarns will help to secure them.

Silk and synthetic yarns

Woollen yarns definitely felt into the fleece far better than silk or synthetic yarns, but you can still use them to decorate your felt. This can be done by placing fleece or woollen yarn over the silk or synthetic yarn to help hold it in place. The effect of mixing different types of yarn is quite interesting. For example, place a bright poppy-red silk yarn in horizontal stripes onto a background of midnight blue carded fleece. Then place a very thin layer of the carded blue fleece over the yarn and the red silk will show through. Next place a very fluffy mohair yarn in vertical stripes in a jade green to make a good contrast in colour to the red and blue. The fleece and the mohair yarn will help to keep the silk in place during the hardening and milling processes. The result is interesting because the silk will not shrink as much as the fleece and will therefore make wavy stripes underneath the fleece and mohair.

Metallic threads

Yarns that are mixed with lurex or thin metallic threads can be combined with the fleece to add sparkle to your felt. Again, trap the threads underneath the fleece or woollen yarn or embroider the top layer of the fleece to hold them in place. This can be achieved by very carefully pulling the thread through the fleece as you would for securing a pattern. The design can be made by using large stitches. This will only work well if you are using a thin smooth yarn. If the thread is too thick and hairy, it will disturb the layers of carded fleece too much. Depending on the type of yarn you are using you may find it better not to make knots or complicated embroidered patterns, as these are less likely to felt in. If you are making felt from black fleece and the last layer is decorated with silk and gold metallic thread, the pattern will look very exotic.

Before placing fancy yarns into your felt, it is a good idea to check for colour fastness and the effect hot water may have on the thread. Some yarns may shrivel up when placed in hot water whilst others may lose a lot of colour. To test how the yarn will react, place a length of yarn into a pot of boiling water before using.

Some suggestions

Study Fig 6 for ideas for placing the yarn on the fleece. Then think about the combinations of colours and textures you want to use that look good with the fleece you are using. The possibilities are endless but here are a few suggestions for colour and texture combinations you may like to try.

✄1 Make up the carded layers of fleece in green. For the final layer blend at the carding stage blue and green with a few splashes of fuchsia pink. Onto this last layer place diagonal stripes across the fleece in bright pink silk thread. Then place thin carded wisps of green fleece randomly over the silk thread. Now make small spirals cut from a random-dyed woollen yarn that is pink, blue and green. Finally, place thin wisps of carded blue fleece over the top of this. The result will be rich in colour and interesting in texture.

✄2 To make a more subtle pattern make up the carded layers in natural coloured fleece. For the top layer card a blend of pale pink and pale blue. Next make a lattice pattern with silver thread diagonally across the fleece. Over this place a thin layer of pale pink fleece so that the silver thread shows through. Then with a fluffy mohair yarn with tufts of mohair in pink, blue and white, make another lattice in horizontal and vertical stripes. Tack the mohair to the fleece and this will hold the silver thread in place. The finished effect will be very soft with a little sparkle of silver showing through.

✄3 If you wish to make a more definite pattern when using yarn then try embroidering a design in the fleece. Make up the carded layers of fleece in fuchsia pink. Then take a silk thread in purple and with large loose stitches make large daisies from chain stitch. Only stitch into the top layer of fleece. Next take a few tufts of yellow fleece and place in the centre of each daisy. Finally take a fluffy mohair yarn in bright green and make a wavy pattern around the daisies. This can be either left as it is or a very thin layer of turquoise placed over the pattern. The combination of different colour fleeces and woollen yarn will fuse together and the silk thread will stand out making an abstract flower motif.

ADDING LACE OR NET INTO THE FELT

The addition of lace or net in your felt will transform the texture of the felt completely. This is not very easy to do and care should be taken when choosing the lace or net. The material needs to be very loosely made with large holes in the pattern and also thin and light. For the material to fuse into the fleece the fibres need to be able to pass through the lace or net to secure it. Cotton lace is less slippery than nylon or a synthetic variety. Good fabric shops and haberdashers now stock a wide range of fancy lace and net. Some designs come in bright colours and others are combined with lurex. For sampling, you can use oddments that you already have. Try using different colours of lace with a variety of different coloured fleece. The combination of fleece and lace will make your felt a lot stronger. The lace or net can be used in two ways: either in cut pieces to make a pattern or in one piece to make a background for a design.

Placing the lace or net on the fleece

Make up the layers of fleece from well-carded fibres and keep the top layer on one side. Then place the lace or net over the fleece and cut to the size of the fleece square. To help keep the lace flat during the hardening process, you will need to secure it. To do this sew with large tacking stitches around the edge of the square and across the square, through the fleece and lace. Now place the final layer of fleece on top. Make sure the final layer is thin and wispy so that the lace shows through. Then you can continue to decorate with yarn or leave it as it is. Cover with a cotton covering and harden by hand and foot. Do not put into the washing machine as the lace will move around too much. It is better to harden the fleece for a long time and make sure the lace or net is felted in before rolling.

If the lace doesn't felt in very well at the hardening stage, then stop and dry the fleece. If the fleece is fairly flat and reasonably matted then you can secure the lace by stitching the layers with a sewing-machine stitch. Sew across the fleece in a quilted formation in either straight stitch or an embroidery stitch. Then cover with the cotton covering and continue hardening. It will be easier to roll the felt with the lace machine stitched in and the finished effect will be quite unusual.

Suggested design for felt with net

If you have chosen a black lace, then use a contrasting background of fleece, ie red. Make up the layers of carded red fleece and decorate with a vivid green mohair yarn in horizontal stripes. Then take the open-patterned black lace and cover the mohair stripes. Next cover with a thin layer of fuchsia pink fleece so that the lace and yarn show through. Either place more yarn over this or leave unpatterned. Secure and cover and harden the fleece. When the felt is made, the complementary colours of red and green will make the mohair pattern distinct. The fuchsia pink fleece will blend with the red to give a vibrant colour, therefore making a feature of the black lace. The whole effect will be very dramatic.

USING WOVEN MATERIAL IN FELT

Combining woven fabric with fleece is more difficult than adding lace. When looking for materials to use, bear in mind that the material must be made with a loose weave and will felt in better if it is made from wool. Silk materials can be used if they are of the right weight and weave. Silk organza and georgette will work better than slippery satins or heavy noils. Therefore choose your materials carefully. You could either use a plain material in a strong colour or a patterned material. This would make a lovely lining to a bag or a pair of slippers. Other gauzy materials could be used, for example, muslin or loosely woven hessian.

There is a variety of ways you can decorate with material. You could either cut patterns or strips of material or cover the whole layer of carded fleece with material and then place another layer of thin carded fleece over this. Alternatively, if you fold the material in half and half again and cut a simple pattern out of the folded material, this will make a holey pattern with the fleece underneath showing through. Another layer of carded fleece will secure the material. To help the material adhere to the fleece, if the material is loosely woven enough, you can pull out some warp or weft threads. This would leave loosely woven gaps in the material allowing the fleece to come through. A feature could be made of this by pulling out the warp and weft threads to produce a checked pattern in the material. Placing another layer of fleece over the top will give the fibres underneath something to adhere to. A combination of fabric and carded stripes of fleece placed over the gaps in the fabric will produce an interesting texture in the felt.

The material will not shrink at the same rate as the wool fibre and this will give a puckered texture. To keep the material flat and to stop it from moving whilst hardening it is necessary to secure it by stitching it into the fleece. A feature can be made of the stitching and it can become a part of the finished design. For example, if a criss-cross stitch is made with embroidery silk through the fabric at 5cm (2in) intervals into

the layers of fleece, the end result will look like seersucker material. The advantage of felting in a material is that it forms a lining and the felt is made stronger. To make the felt, cover the fleece with a cotton covering and pat well at the hardening stage before stamping. Roll the felt once the material has adhered to the fleece.

Suggested design

Make up the carded layers in bright blue. Take a piece of red silk organza cut to the size of the fleece square. Fold the silk into four and cut out a triangle on a folded edge – the unfolded material will show a diamond pattern – and the blue fleece will show through the cut-out diamonds. Now cover the surface with a thin layer of yellow loose tacking stitches. Cover with a cotton covering and continue with the hardening and milling process. When the felt is fully made the yellow fleece will blend with the blue fleece making it slightly green. The yellow fleece over the red fabric will make the red appear slightly orange. The finished result will be an interesting combination of colours and textures.

USING KNITTING

A good material to felt into your fleece is knitting and this is more likely to be successful than a woven material. When sampling with different yarns you will find some that felt in very well. It is worth using these yarns to knit up into small sample-size squares. Try out different knitting patterns using either a very lacy design or large needles to produce a loose knit. The knitted square could be made from a woollen yarn or a fluffy mohair. Multicoloured or textured yarns will look particularly good. Knit the square to approximately the same size as your carded layers. Or, alternatively, knit strips to make knitted stripes. Do not stretch the knitting to fit the fleece as it will only shrink back and pucker the surface of the fleece.

To cover the whole surface of carded fleece, take a square of lacy knitting and smooth it over the fleece. Stitch the knitting to the carded layers with large tacking stitches around the edge of the square and diagonally across. Cover over with the cotton covering and follow the hardening and milling procedure. When using strips of knitting sew on each individual stripe.

Instead of knitting, loose crochet can be used. Alternatively, you could weave a square leaving gaps between the yarn and place on the fleece. Whether using knitting, crochet or weaving the design must be made loosely using soft yarn to ensure it will felt in successfully. If you can spin, use your own yarn spun

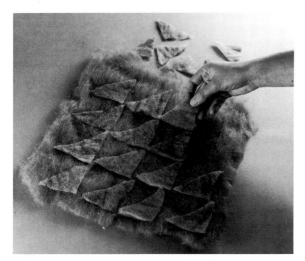

✂ **Plates 29-32** Decorating with patterned felt: (from top left) decorating the first layer; decorating the last layer; half-made felt shapes; finished piece decorated with yarn

from the fleece you are using and then knit, crochet or weave it.

Suggested design

Make up the carded layers in grey, making the top layer a blend of grey and pink fleece. Loosely knit, crochet or weave a square in lilac woollen yarn and place onto the top layer. With a needle and thread, tack with large, loose stitches around the square attaching it to the fleece. For added decoration, when there are intersections in the knitted, crocheted or woven square, embroider star shapes with a pale pink silk thread using long stitches. Carefully stitch over the knitting through into the fleece. Cover over with a cotton covering and continue to harden and mill. The finished piece will be a subtle mixture of colours. The grey and pink background will make a feature of the knitted, crocheted or woven square and the silk thread will highlight the design.

HOW TO MAKE DEFINED SHAPES WITH FLEECE

Having tried methods of decorating the fleece with yarn or materials that produce a geometric or abstract effect, you may decide you want to produce a pattern that is more defined. Tufts of fleece can be used to make a multicoloured spotty surface but perhaps you want to make clean cut patterns of squares, triangles, circles or flowers.

This can be done quite easily but it is necessary to make some half-made felt first. To make the half-made felt, it has to be made from a couple of layers of well-carded fleece. The half-made felt has to be thin so as not to make the finished felt uneven. Make up sample-size pieces of felt from either one colour or a colour blend or a different colour for each layer but use a maximum of three layers of fleece. Cover the fleece with a cotton covering and sprinkle with hot water and pat until the fleece becomes compressed but not fully felted. When the fibres are reasonably adhered but still loose enough to pull apart, carefully remove the cotton covering. Remove the half-made felt, trying not to make holes, and dry flat.

It is worth making up lots of pieces of half-made felt in different colours. These thin layers of carded fleece can all be covered over separately but hardened at the same time. By placing them one on top of the other

Fig 7 Using half-made felt shapes: circles; squares; triangles; leaves; flowers; and a combination of shapes

the pressure of your hands will slightly felt all the pieces at once.

Once the half-made felt is dry, you can cut out the shapes you want to use (see Fig 7). Geometric shapes are good and can either be placed in a regular pattern or used abstractly to form stylised flowers or fruits. Once you have tried some simple designs, you will have lots of ideas for a design that is more complex. Start by sampling with lots of different shapes and colours. Make up carded layers of fleece for six samples of different colours and then make a different pattern on each piece.

Patterns using squares

Cut lots of squares from one piece of half-made felt about 5cm (2in) square. These can either be placed onto the top layer of carded fleece at regular intervals to make a checked pattern or placed at random. Play around with placing the squares in different ways. Ideally, you want to use half-made felt of a contrasting colour to your fleece background to make a feature of the pattern. If you find the size of the square restricting then cut the occasional square into four little squares of 2.5cm (1in) to make a pattern of different sized squares. When you have decided on the pattern layout, take a needle and thread and tack the squares

to the fleece. Cover with the cotton covering and harden and mill the fleece.

Triangles

By cutting your squares in half you can make regular-shaped triangles. The triangles could be used alongside the squares or on their own. Alternatively, a less geometric pattern could be made from the half-made felt by cutting irregular triangles, perhaps small fat ones or tall thin ones. Decide whether you want your pattern to be very regular or more abstract. Triangles can be used to make stylised flower motifs. Lots of small thin triangles can be used to make up the petals of a flower and larger ones placed to look like leaves. Two regular equilateral triangles overlapped will make a six-pointed star.

Circles

To cut regular-sized neat round circles from your half-made felt, it helps to have a shape to draw around. Use a cup or similar vessel as a pattern. Place the cup onto the half-made felt and draw round with tailor's chalk. Then cut out the neat circle. Cut lots of circles of different sizes and they can be used to form a pattern of spots or mixed with squares and triangles to make an abstract geometric design. If you are making stylised flowers, a circle can be used for the centre of the flower. Circles can be made to look like fruits, eg a bunch of grapes, apples, oranges or cherries.

You will soon find that from these basic geometric shapes there is plenty of scope for design, either using the shapes mixed together or on their own. Of course, you do not have to keep to these shapes. To make flower patterns from half-made felt, look at an individual flower. Cut pieces of half-made felt to the pattern of the petals and do the same with the leaves. Butterflies are interesting shapes to copy to pattern your felt. Look around your home and garden for other ideas for interesting shapes.

Stripes of half-made felt can be cut with wavy or zigzag edges or a whole piece of half-made felt can be folded and a pattern cut out to make a stencilled design. In fact, the half-made felt can be cut to any shape you want and the clean-cut edge will give you a well-defined shape. Once the design has been placed onto the fleece it must be secured with tacking stitches before covering and hardening.

The advantage of making a design with half-made felt is that you can put the design onto the felt to make a motif for a pocket or a border for a waistcoat. It will also make the finished piece of felt look more controlled. Once the piece of felt has been made, the pattern can be enhanced with machine or hand embroidery.

Suggested design

It is a good exercise to make a piece of felt with a design made from a variety of shapes cut from half-made felt. Make up the carded layers in a deep midnight blue. Next take a piece of fuchsia half-made felt and cut lots of 4cm (1½in) long thin triangles. Use to make the petals of a flower motif. To make the centre of each flower, cut 2.5cm (1in) circles of yellow half-made felt. Place five fuchsia-pink triangles in a circle with the points facing inwards and lay the yellow circle over the points to make the centre. To make the leaves, cut leaf shapes from half-made green felt and place around the flowers. Frame the flowers with a border by cutting 5cm (2in) strips of half-made green felt and cut with a zigzag edge. Place this around the edge of the blue fleece to frame the flowers. Secure the pattern and cover with a cotton cloth and follow the hardening and milling procedure. This could be made into a wall-hanging or used as a pocket.

It is possible to mix yarn with half-made felt shapes. An alternative way to decorate the felt would be to cover the background fleece with lace or net and then make a pattern with half-made felt shapes. The more you put into the felt, the more interesting the finished piece will be.

When deciding what pattern to make, it is helpful to draw some ideas on paper and then cut these out and place onto the fleece. Once you have decided on the design, use the paper shapes as templates and place onto the half-made felt and cut out the shapes you want. Remember it is possible to place a pattern on both sides of the felt. Make lots of samples before you start making large pieces of patterned felt (see Chapter 7 for ways to use your samples).

MIXING THE DIFFERENT METHODS

The next stage of making patterned felt is to mix the different methods of making a design. You may like to try out some of these ideas of combining lace, yarn and half-made felt shapes.

Suggested design (1)

✂1 To make a pattern from a combination of yarns and geometric shapes in half-made felt, start by making up the carded layers in green fleece. Make the top layer a blend of green and blue fleece mixed whilst carding. This will make the background more interesting.

✂2 Next take two types of yarn, one smooth thick red woollen yarn and the other a fluffy mohair black yarn. Cut the yarn into lengths long enough to make a lattice pattern in both colours on the carded fleece.

✂3 From half-made felt in dark blue and yellow cut

5cm (2in) squares from the blue and 5cm (2in) diameter circles from the yellow. Place the blue squares at regular spaced intervals across the carded fleece background and over the yarn.

✄4 Take the black and red yarn and make stripes over the blue squares but in between the first placed stripes of yarn.

✄5 Finish off the pattern by placing the yellow circles inbetween the squares and over the yarn.

✄6 With a needle and thread, secure the pattern with large stitches. By stitching down the circles and squares you will also be securing the yarn.

✄7 Cover with a cotton covering and harden and mill the felt in the usual way.

This will make a vibrant multicoloured geometric patterned felt. Where the half-made felt shapes cover the yarn the texture of the yarn will show through. The different layers of pattern will give depth to the design in the felt.

Suggested design (2)

This is a softer and more subtle pattern from a combination of yarn and half-made felt shapes.

✄1 Make up the carded layers in a natural coloured fleece.

✄2 Take a soft fluffy yarn in pastel colours and make a spiral pattern with the yarn on the carded fleece.

✄3 Take some half-made felt in pale pink, pale blue and soft grey, and cut lots of little triangles 5cm (2in) high with a 2.5cm (1in) base.

✄4 Place the triangles randomly over the spiral pattern and secure them with large tacking stitches which will also secure the yarn.

✄5 Cover with a cotton cloth and continue to harden and mill.

The natural-coloured fleece background will make the colour of the triangles much softer and the fluffy yarn spiral will only show through where there are no triangles. The finished piece of felt will be a soft mixture of colours in an abstract design.

Suggested design (3)

This is a more complicated design, using lace in the background and then a pattern of yarn and half-made felt shapes.

✄1 Make up the carded layers in red fleece.

✄2 Cut black open-patterned lace to a size to cover the red fleece.

✄3 Take a fluffy blue yarn and make diagonal stripes across the lace about 4cm (1½in) apart.

✄4 From the half-made red felt cut small diamond stripes and place along the blue yarn at regular intervals. Cover the whole area in this way.

✄5 Stitch through the diamond shapes into the lace and fleece. This will keep the lace and yarn in place.

✄6 Cover with a cotton cloth to protect the design and harden and mill the felt.

The red fleece will make a good background for the black lace and the blue yarn will stand out well against the red. The red diamond shapes could look like shapes cut out of the lace and also help trap the lace into the felt. This is a good combination of colours and textures.

Suggested design (4)

To produce a design of defined stylised flowers it is possible to use the yarn to make details on the flowers, eg to make the pattern of the stem and stamens in the centre of the flower. For a dramatic effect use carded layers of black fleece speckled with red, yellow and green silk fibre.

✄1 Make the speckles by cutting tiny amounts of silk fibre and sprinkle over the black fleece.

✄2 To make a bottom edge to the pattern, cut a 5cm (2in) wide strip of green half-made felt.

✄3 On one side of this strip cut out long thin triangles to make a spikey edge. Place this at the bottom of the square of carded fleece.

✄4 Take the long thin triangles in green and place them over the rest of the fleece with the points facing upwards. This will make a background of grass.

✄5 From the red half-made felt cut eight rounded poppy-shaped petals and place onto the fleece to make two flower motifs.

✄6 With a green fluffy yarn make the stems by hiding one end under the petals and the other end of the yarn under the green border.

✄7 From the green half-made felt cut a few leaf shapes and place on either side of the stems.

✄8 To make a centre to the poppies make small pom-pons from yellow yarn. Do not make the pom-pons too thick and place in the centre of the poppies.

✄9 To finish off the poppies, cut two small circles from black half-made felt and place over the yellow pom-pons, allowing the yellow yarn to spray out.

✄10 Stitch all the detail to the fleece, cover with a cotton cloth and follow the hardening and milling procedure.

This design makes a lovely picture and could be used either as a wall-hanging to be enhanced with embroidery or as a pocket on a jacket.

These are only a few ideas to show you what you can do with patterned felt. Start by making simple patterns and work up to producing a complicated design. That way you will know where extra care is needed when designing and securing the pattern.

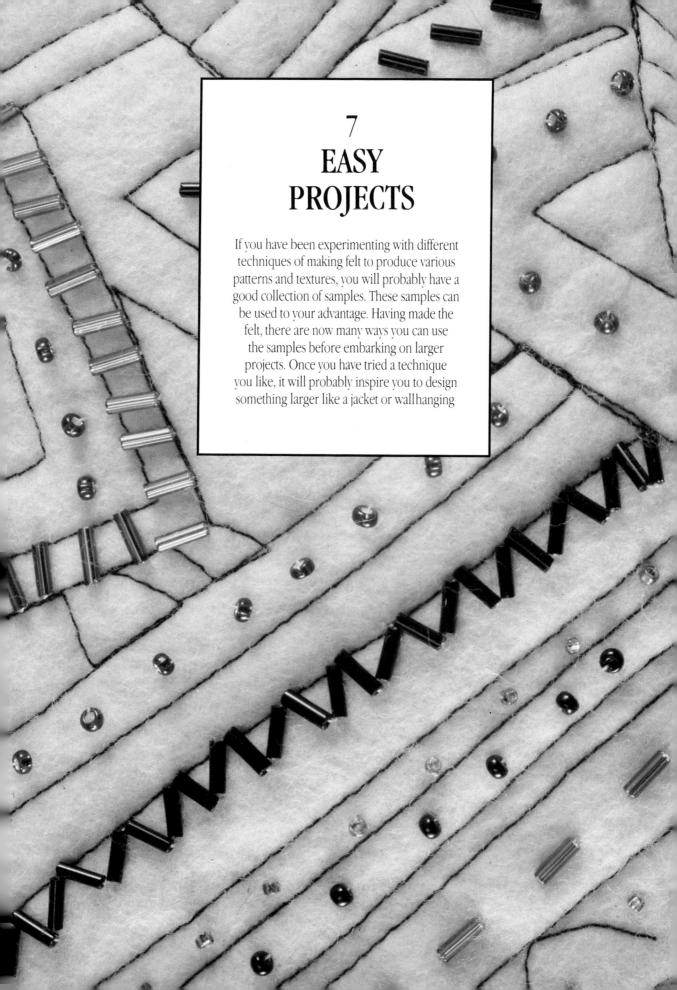

7
EASY PROJECTS

If you have been experimenting with different techniques of making felt to produce various patterns and textures, you will probably have a good collection of samples. These samples can be used to your advantage. Having made the felt, there are now many ways you can use the samples before embarking on larger projects. Once you have tried a technique you like, it will probably inspire you to design something larger like a jacket or wall hanging

Perhaps you prefer making smaller items like toys, bags or hats, therefore sample-size pieces of felt will be large enough for what you need.

MAKING USE OF FELT BALLS

During each felt-making session you will have probably accumulated oddments of fleece which are probably not enough in quantity to make a piece of felt. They can be used to make felt balls (as described in Chapter 4) which are so easy to make that it is worth making lots of them. By varying the size and colour of the felt balls you will have a good variety to design with. Children in particular will enjoy making felt balls and what can be made from them.

Making fruits

Making fruit shapes from felt balls is great fun and very easy. If your felt balls have been made from multicoloured fleece, this will give the fruit a more interesting appearance. For example, if you are making apples, then a mixture of red, yellow and green fleece would be suitable. Lots of little red felt balls can be made into clusters of cherries. To make a bunch of grapes, take lots of felt balls, either in one colour or mixed, and try sewing them together very closely. Individual fruits like strawberries can be made by sewing tiny beads into the felt ball to give the appearance of seeds. Use a short-staple fleece for a smooth appearance to fruit. Small pieces of felt cut from the edges of your felt samples can be used to make leaves and stems.

It is worthwhile making as many different fruits as you like. You can decide later what to do with them. Until you use them, place them together in a bowl. You may decide you like them so much as an ornament you won't want to use them for anything else.

Making insects

Making insects from felt is just as easy as making fruit. Bumble bees can be made from a mixture of black and yellow felt balls. Sew three together tightly to form the body. To make the wings, cut two small oval pieces of net and stitch them onto the back of the body in the centre. Sew on tiny beads or sequins for eyes. For a hairy bumble bee use felt balls made from a long-staple fleece and brush with a wire brush to make them look fluffy. Little flies can be made in a similar way, but using only one felt ball rolled and squashed into a oval. By using embroidery thread, it is possible to divide the body into three sections and then add details of the eyes and wings. To make longer bodies for dragonflies and butterflies, cut a strip of felt approximately 4cm (2in) x 2cm (1in) and roll the felt

very tightly. Secure the roll of felt with small stitches along the cut edge. By using embroidery thread and beads, patterns on the body can be made. The wings can be made from net or thin felt or even other materials like silk.

It is a good idea to use paintings and photographs of insects for reference for colour and shapes. There is no reason why you shouldn't invent your own insects and base the shape of the body and wings on the real thing.

Multicoloured caterpillars can be fun to make for children and pets. To make one simply sew a number of different-coloured felt balls together tightly with beads for eyes. If you use rolled elastic instead of cotton, this will make the caterpillar more fun to play with.

Note: If you intend to make any felt items for children, you must make sure that all beads are sewn on tightly. Also some felt remains hairy if the fleece has a long staple so avoid using this to make toys for small children or animals, as they may try to eat it.

Making flowers

Other attractive items which can be made from felt balls and scraps of felt are flowers. The felt ball forms the centre of the flower and segments of small pieces of felt make the petals. By sewing the petals onto one side of the felt ball, it will appear that the petals are growing out from the centre of the ball. The petals can be cut in any shape or size. Indeed, a flower can be made from felt petals alone. To make the petals look more delicate use felt made from a combination of short-staple fleece and unspun silk fibre. The flowers will then look silky and soft.

A flower can be made by placing together a number of small felt triangles with cut fringed edges that are rolled into a cone. Secure the petals with small stitches to make a bell-shaped flower. The leaves can be cut from small pieces of felt that are then sewn onto the flower. A few flowers can be sewn together with leaves inbetween to make a spray.

Studying photographs or paintings of flowers or the real thing is helpful. This will give you ideas for the shape of the petals and how to construct the flower. The use of beading and embroidery can pick out details of stamens and patterns on your flowers.

Jewellery

Turning felt-ball designs into jewellery is an ideal way to make use of them. The individual fruits, insects and flowers can be used separately or clustered together. Sew a safety pin or brooch pin onto the back of the decoration to make a very simple but effective brooch. An attractive and unusual necklace can easily be made

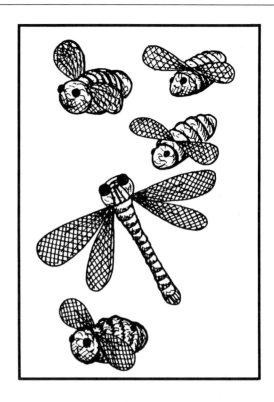

Fig 8 Mobile designs: fruits; insects; flowers; animals

by threading together a line of felt balls onto rolled elastic or fishing line. Then as a centrepiece to the necklace attach an insect, flower or fruit, or perhaps all three. Thread on a few more felt balls to make the necklace long enough to get over your head, then tie the ends of the elastic or fishing line together. Bracelets can be made in a similar way by adding long thin stitched rolls of felt between the felt balls. A combination of wooden beads and felt decorations works quite well. Good craft shops often sell beads and fastenings for making jewellery. To match a necklace why not make a pair of earrings by sewing an ear wire to a fruit or insect. Felt jewellery is great fun to make and looks very attractive when worn on jackets, jumpers and hats.

Toys

As felt balls are easy for children to make, it seems natural to use them to make toys. Use the balls as soft marbles or counters on board games. It is possible to make little felt men and women in a similar way to caterpillars. Use different size and colour felt balls for different parts of the body, eg make legs by threading together little felt balls on rolled elastic or fishing line. Use a large blue ball for the body. Make arms from small yellow balls and the head from a large felt ball in natural off-white fleece. Small offcuts of felt can be used to make hands, feet and hats for the characters. The facial features can be made with beads and embroidery stitches. With imagination, little felt animals can be made in a similar way. By adding small pieces of felt in the shape of ears and tails little mice are easy to make.

Mobiles

If you are making felt toys for very small children, then mobiles are a good way to display the characters you have made. Small children are often not content with just handling objects and may try and eat them as well. By making a mobile, the decorations can still be enjoyed but will be safely out of reach. Mobiles also make good presents.

Mobiles are very easy to make: all you need are two pieces of wood, more if you want a larger mobile, and fishing line. Make a cross with the lengths of wood and bind with the fishing line. Then the characters can be threaded onto the nylon line and hung from the piece of wood. Hang as many characters as you like to make a well-balanced mobile and finally make a loop in the centre of the cross of wood to hang the mobile from the ceiling. If the mobile is hung by a window, it will move around.

 **Colour Plate 12** Felt and felt-ball decorations

FELT BUTTONS

Making felt buttons is an ideal way of using the edges of your felt samples left over after trimming. These scraps of felt can be turned into very attractive buttons that resemble sweets. All you need is a strip of felt 15cm (6in) x 1.25cm (½in). Simply coil the felt strip around itself as tightly as you can to make a spiral circle of felt. Then place a pin through the coil to hold it in place. Take a needle and thread and stitch through all the layers of felt from one side through to the other. It is possible to vary the size of the button by changing the length and width of the strip of felt. If you are using felt made from different-coloured layers of fleece this will make a lovely multicoloured button.

USING FELT FOR PATCHWORK

If you do feel very worried about cutting your felt samples into smaller pieces, an ideal item to make is a patchwork quilt. By simply trimming your samples into squares of equal size (keep the edges for buttons, etc) you can add to the quilt as you make more samples. Therefore this could be an ongoing project. If you keep all your samples to approximately the same size, you will be able to make a very regular patchwork pattern. If they vary in size it doesn't really matter, but you will have to juggle the squares of felt around to fit them together.

You have two options when using your samples to make a quilt. Either you can make the patchwork very regular and geometric by trimming all the samples to the same size, or you may prefer the irregular fluffy edges that naturally remain on the felt sample. If you keep the raw edges, a feature can be made of these.

Sewing the patchwork together

There are several ways you can sew together the pieces of patchwork. Which way you choose will depend on the effect you want to achieve. Machine stitching could be used on the right or wrong side. Invisible hand stitching could be used so as not to distract from the felt or the edges could be exaggerated with the use of hand embroidery. Of course, you could use a combination of hand and machine stitching. What method you decide to use will depend on how long you want to spend making the quilt and which technique you prefer.

If you decide to make a quilt from regular trimmed squares of felt, then these may look better machine stitched together. A feature can be made of the sample edges by making an ordinary flat seam but with the pressed seam being shown on the outside of the quilt. Hand embroidery could be used on the corners. Alter-natively you could embroider the squares together using cross-stitch.

If you decide to keep the samples with their natural irregular edges, the easiest way to join the samples is by overlapping them and securing with invisible hand stitching. Alternatively, overlap the edges of two samples, stitch in place, then enhance the edge with hand embroidery following the line of the edge.

Cutting different patchwork motifs

Squares. If you decide you like the idea of making a patchwork pattern with your felt, but prefer a smaller patchwork design, then simply cut your felt samples into smaller squares of regular size. To make the design more unusual cut the sample into four pieces. This will give you four squares each with two neat sides and two irregular edges. If you cut the samples into four even-sized squares, you can always vary the design by cutting one square into four again. This way you could end up with large and small squares that will fit together easily but vary the design.

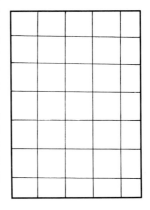 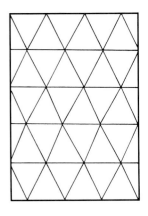

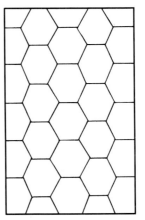 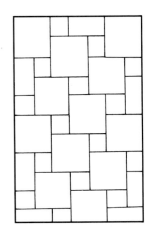

✂ **Fig 9** Patchwork motifs: squares; triangles; hexagons; large and small squares

60

Triangles. This is a simple shape to use. The easiest way to make triangles of regular shape and size is to cut a square in half diagonally and then in half again to make smaller regular triangles. If you use the same dimensions for your squares and triangles it is possible to use both shapes in your patchwork.

Using traditional patchwork motifs

You may well prefer to make a more traditional design using traditional patchwork motifs. Templates can be bought from craftshops or you can make your own from card. Traditional patchwork patterns rely upon the shapes being regular so that the pieces fit together neatly to produce a pattern. You will not be able to make a patchwork with felt in the same way you would with cotton material. Felt is too thick to turn back the edges and this is a waste of time anyway because felt does not fray.

Motifs used for traditional patchwork also include octagons, hexagons and diamonds. By clever planning on paper, a combination of shapes can be fitted together.

If you do not have the patience to wait for your patchwork to grow into a quilt to cover a bed or chair, you can use smaller pieces to make other things. By making smaller pieces you can try out different combinations of shapes and colours.

Cushions

Cushions are an ideal way of displaying your patchwork designs. Very quickly you can see your felt turning into something useful that will be admired. Gradually you can build up a collection of cushions made from your own felt. These will look attractive grouped together on a sofa or bed.

To make your felt go as far as possible, it makes sense to produce the patchwork design on the front of the cushion, then the back panel can be made out of a complementary material. Base the size of your cushion on the size of the pad you will fill it with. When sewing the cover onto the pad, make sure you use a method which will enable you to remove the cover for washing when necessary.

Seat covers

Along similar lines to making a cushion a piece of patchwork felt could be used to cover the seat of a chair instead of furnishing fabric. The piece of patchwork will need to be large enough to generously cover the seat of the chair, stretched and tacked into place, and the excess felt trimmed away. To cover the tacks, strips of felt can be stitched around the edge of the chair onto the seat of felt. If you do not have enough felt use braid from a furnishing shop.

Accessories and garments

Small bags and purses are ideal small objects to make from pieces of patchwork. The patchwork can be built up to make the shape of the bag or purse and therefore can be as large or as small as you want it to be. It then helps to draw the finished design onto paper to the size of the finished object. This will give you something to use as a guide whilst making the patchwork.

Depending on how ambitious you are you could build up your patchwork pieces of felt to make a waistcoat or jacket. This obviously takes a lot more planning and a pattern is essential to work on. The pattern acts as your guide to make sure that all your patchwork pieces will fit together well on the garment.

If you start by making something simple like a cushion or bag, you will have an idea of how difficult it will be to make a garment. Advance planning of the design is essential and always helps in the long run.

WEAVING WITH FELT STRIPS

Using felt strips to weave with produces a patchwork-like effect but is more interesting because it looks three-dimensional. Sample-size pieces of felt are ideal to use to try this technique. It doesn't matter if your felt is natural, coloured, plain or patterned. Indeed a mix of all these types of felt will make the design more interesting.

You will need a ruler, tailor's chalk, pins, scissors and a variety of felt. Take one piece of felt and trim it into a regular square or rectangle. Trimming away the flimsy edges will leave the felt of uniform thickness which is much better for this technique. Using tailor's chalk and a ruler, divide the piece of felt lengthways into four, equal-size long fat strips. Then cut the strips of felt. Take two strips and place onto a flat surface in a horizontal position. Place the third strip at 90° to the first two and weave it over and under the felt. Weave the fourth strip of felt under and over the first two strips and underneath the third. Pin the strips into place. You will have a very basic woven design.

By trying this very simple weaving technique you will understand how it works. If you then unpin the four strips and cut them in half lengthways, you will have eight thinner strips. Use these to weave in the same way – four horizontally and four vertically. This will make a square of woven felt but will leave lengths of felt loose around the square. This can be used as a base for a wall hanging and the loose ends can be made into loops, or twisted or woven back into the design.

To produce a regular square of flat interwoven strips, you may need to cut two squares of felt into even widths and then weave them together.

Example

Take two pieces of felt and cut each sample into a 25cm (10in) square. Then with tailor's chalk divide the squares into ten strips 2cm (1in) wide x 25cm (10in). Cut out the strips of felt from both pieces of felt so that you have twenty strips. Place ten strips of felt together in a square in a horizontal direction and then one by one weave the other ten strips vertically across, pinning as you go. This will produce a pattern of squares.

Variation

To make a more interesting pattern, try varying the way the strips are woven. Instead of going over one under one, try going over two under one. Remember to move along a space each time. The first three rows would be as follows with ten strips:

✁1 Over one under two, over one under two, over one under two, over one.
✁2 Over two under one, over two under one, over two under one, over one.
✁3 Over one under two, over one under two, over one under two, over one
✁4 As step 2.

    Continue in this formation until all the felt strips have been woven. This will produce an interesting pattern of rectangles and squares.

To make the woven strips more interesting

To make the pattern more interesting there are several things you can do. The most obvious is to use contrasting colours of felt. If you take two samples of felt in different colours and then cut into strips and weave them the pattern will be more apparent.

    If you are using patterned felt samples, the colour may be different on each side giving you four colours to weave with. Another way to add interest to the woven pattern is to use strips of felt in varying widths (see Fig 10 and Colour Plate 13). A combination of different colours and widths will produce a design that has areas of different sizes and colours formed in a regular pattern. There are so many different woven patterns that can be made from this technique.

How to secure the woven strips

Depending on what you intend to do with the woven felt you will need to secure the strips to keep the pattern. Pinning the strips as you weave them assures that the finished design is held in place. Secure the strips permanently by using machine or hand stitching. Machine stitching will give the woven strips a quilted appearance and enhance the design. If you use hand stitching it means the strips can be sewn

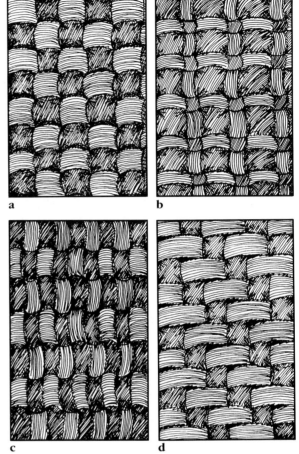

✁ **Fig 10** Woven strip designs: a) even-cut lengths; b) thick and thin strips; c) thick in one direction only; d) an alternative weave

together invisibly so that they still appear loosely woven. With the addition of hand embroidery areas of the woven design can be tucked, twisted and bound.

How to use the woven design

There are several ways you can use the woven felt strip designs. The weaving can be used as a design in its own right to be made into a wall hanging or table decoration. There is no reason why the woven design cannot be made into a bag. This technique is ideal for making cushions but not suitable for making garments as the loose woven areas are likely to catch. Hats can be made from this technique, however, and any loose ends could be made a feature of.

MAKING A WALLHANGING OR COLLAGE

As sampling leaves you with a variety of pieces of felt of different colours and textures, a good item to make is a collage or wallhanging on which you can keep all

your samples together. This will be useful as a source of reference.

When designing a wallhanging it helps to have a source of reference for inspiration. Therefore start by deciding what design you want to make in detail. This can be geometric or pictorial or a combination of the two. The size of your wallhanging will depend on the amount of samples you have available. A good idea, maybe, is to make a series of small designs based on a particular theme. Then you can add to the designs as you make more samples.

If you decide to make one large wallhanging you will need a different material to use as your background to place the felt on. The background could be hard, ie wood or cork, or soft, ie hessian or silk. The background you decide upon will depend upon the design you have chosen. The background needs to be sympathetic to the actual design in colour and texture.

You will also need to consider how to fix the felt to

✄ **Colour Plate 13** Weaving with strips of felt

the background. If you have chosen a hardwood as background then you will probably have to use a multi-purpose glue to stick the felt down. If you are using cork or a soft board then it is possible to pin the pattern into place. The design could be enhanced with the use of pins, drawings pins, tacks or staples. However, if you use a soft material background it will be possible to machine or hand stitch the pieces of felt into place and complement the pattern with hand or machine embroidery.

When you have decided on the design and the background, it will be necessary to make a paper pattern. Make a drawing on paper to the size of the intended finished design. This will then show you all the shapes you will need to cut from your felt samples so that you can check you have enough felt. It will also help you to decide how you fit the pieces of felt together, therefore you are less likely to make mistakes and waste any felt unnecessarily.

When you have made the paper pattern design, it is a good idea to duplicate it. You can then cut the copy up into the individual shapes. It will probably help to number the pieces that you cut up to correspond with the original paper design. This will save you getting the shapes in a muddle and you will know exactly where to place each piece of felt. The individual pieces of the pattern can be pinned onto the felt samples when you have decided on colours. Once all the pieces have been allocated to a piece of felt all the shapes can be cut out.

One of the advantages of felt here is that the edges do not fray so therefore you will not need to cover them or finish them in any way. If you are using felt made from many different-coloured layers a feature can be made of this. Once all the pieces have been cut out they can be assembled on the background. If you are making small individual designs one sample-size piece of felt may make a good background. If you have any felt samples that are mistakes or didn't felt properly, you may be able to incorporate them into your wallhanging design. A piece of felt with holes in can look very interesting placed over another piece of felt or with the background showing through.

A wallhanging doesn't have to be made from flat pieces of felt. You could also use felt balls to make a three-dimensional surface. Strips or pieces of felt can be pleated, tucked or folded to produce a relief surface. When designing a flat surface, there is no reason why you shouldn't bring a piece of felt out of the picture to add a three-dimensional effect.

A relief surface design

Another way of producing a relief surface is to use layers of felt. The relief surface can be built up by placing one layer of felt on top of another layer. This can produce an interesting effect particularly when using contrasting colours and a mixture of shapes. To exaggerate the three-dimensional effect the shapes can be padded with fleece. One way of doing this is to sew or staple the shape onto the background and leave a small opening through which to push the fleece. Depending on how soft or hard you want the piece to be keep adding fleece until the pattern is full enough to hold its shape. By doing this in certain areas you can make patches of quilted texture. It is also possible to produce a design based on a face. The relief of the face can be built up in this way.

POCKETS

Pockets can be made the full size of the sample or far smaller and in any shape or size. There is no reason why you shouldn't have a round, triangular or square pocket or even one in the shape of a fish. If you have tried making a pocket in one piece with no seams you will have a sample that could be enhanced with some decoration.

A pocket can be made to be sewn onto a garment or to hang from a belt or jacket or even on a wall hanging. A good way to start making pockets is to make lots of paper patterns of different shapes and sizes. Then if you have a certain garment in mind the paper pattern pocket can be tried against the jumper or jacket to check if the design is suitable.

If your sample pieces of felt are of natural-coloured fleece you may want to decorate the pocket with hand or machine embroidery before sewing it on. On the other hand, if your samples of felt are patterned and coloured you will probably want to make a feature of the pocket on the garment and therefore choose the colour and shape accordingly.

Patch pocket

When making a patch pocket, whatever the size or shape, it is necessary to decide what to do with the edges. If your felt sample is made from multicoloured layers of fleece you may want to make a feature of the edges. When the pocket is sewn on the raw edges of the felt it will show the different coloured layers. When showing the raw edge of a piece of felt it is necessary to make sure the edge has been cut neatly and smoothly. To help open out the raw edge to display the different-coloured layers, machine stitch around the pocket 0.5cm (¼in) from the edge. This will help to strengthen the edge as well as display the colours. The pocket can then be sewn onto the garment following the same line of machine stitching leaving the opening at the top or side.

You may of course not want to make a feature of the edges and prefer to have turned edges. When cutting the pocket from the sample of felt a seam allowance must be cut around the whole pattern. A good-size seam allowance for turning is 1.25cm (½in). If you are using a piece of felt that has a different colour or pattern on each side then this can be used to add decoration to the pocket. When the pocket has been cut out work around the edge pinning back the allowance making sure to turn the corners to make as neat as possible. Replace the pins with tacking stitches to keep the turned edge in place and then machine stitch close to the raw edge and close to the folded edge. You will then have a pocket with a neatly turned edge with two rows of machine stitching. When you come to sew the pocket onto the garment you will have a choice of which way to sew the pocket on. The pocket could be sewn on with the turned edge inwards and concealed or with the turned edge outwards. This would give the pocket a border of another colour.

Before you sew a pocket onto the garment it is worth playing around with the position of the pocket. You may find it looks better sewn on at an angle. Once you have decided on the position of the pocket it can then be pinned into place. It isn't necessary to machine stitch the pocket in place and if you have decorated the pocket with embroidery it may look better to use embroidery stitches to secure it. If you are placing a pocket onto a jumper you may well find it easier to hand stitch the pocket.

Another way to edge a pocket is to bind the edge. This can look very attractive particularly if the pocket has been lined. First line the pocket by placing the felt pocket onto the chosen lining material and cut out the exact shape. Then pin and stitch the pocket to the lining with a line of stitches close to the edge. Now cut strips of bias binding from the lining material and sew onto the edge of the pocket to cover all raw edges. Sew onto the garment in a similar way to the raw-edge pocket. Strips of felt can also be used to cover the edges. If the edging felt is a contrasting colour it will look attractive as well as adding strength.

Free-hanging pocket

If you decide to make a free-hanging pocket you will need a back and a front to the pocket. The whole pocket can be made of felt or half felt and half material. If you are using all felt you could change the pattern and colour of each side to make it reversible. If you choose to back the pocket with another material the fabric will have to be of a similar weight to the felt to make the pocket hang correctly.

A free-hanging pocket can be made with or without a concealed seam. Therefore if you are making a concealed seam you will need to make a seam allowance when cutting out the two pieces of the pocket. If you are making a feature of the raw edges you do not need a seam allowance. This type of pocket can be finished off in the same way as a patch pocket.

The idea of a free-hanging pocket is that it can be worn when needed and removed when necessary. Therefore the way it is fixed to the garment has to be considered. One way of joining a pocket to a garment would be to place two or more button holes in the pocket and buttons on the garment where it is to be placed. Alternatively, rouleau loops made from material or felt can be sewn to the top edge of the

pocket and fixed to the garment by means of buttons or felt balls. By using either of these two methods you would be making a feature of the fixing method on the garment and the pocket.

If you want to use a more invisible method to secure the pocket then hooks and eyes could be used. Velcro and press-studs also make the pocket easy to remove, but they do not look so attractive when the pocket isn't in place.

A belt made from felt with removable pockets is a very simple garment to make from your sample. It is also a good-size item to make before making a waistcoat or jacket. These pockets could also be used on a wall hanging for more practical purposes such as holding dressmaking equipment or stationery.

BAGS

Making small simple bags is really an extension of making pockets. Chapter 8 shows patterns for making bags but they can be as simple as you like. A bag can be made from one piece of felt and therefore your felt samples are ideal. A small bag can be made from a piece of felt 30cm (12in) x 10cm (4in). This strip of felt can have the bottom two-thirds folded to make the bag and the remaining third makes the flap to cover the opening. The flap can be left square or the corners can be cut off to make a semi-circle or be cut into an arrow shape. By varying the dimensions of the piece of felt and the shape of the covering flap many different-shaped bags can be made using this method. There are only two seams on this type of bag and these can be either made a feature of or concealed. The edges can be finished off in the same way as the pockets. Then all you need to do is to decide whether the bag needs a strap so it can be worn over the shoulder and what type of fastening. To turn the bag into a shoulder bag a strap can be made from strips of felt sewn together or a braid can be used instead.

Larger bags can be made from several felt samples. A multicoloured bag can be made from three different coloured samples of felt, using one colour for the front, another for the back and a third for the closing flap. If a bag is being made from three pieces the bottom of the bag can be shaped in a semi-circle or whatever shape is desired. All types of fastenings can be used to keep the bag closed. A square of velcro is very quick and easy to sew on. Press-studs, hooks and eyes or buttons are also ideal, but a really fun thing to do is to use your felt decorations as a feature on the bag.

MAKING USE OF FELT DECORATIONS ON GARMENTS AND BAGS

When you have made the felt samples into something, be it a bag, a hat or a wallhanging, any of the felt decorations you have made can be used to decorate the articles.

When making a fastening on a bag, felt balls are ideal to use instead of buttons and look far more interesting. A loop made from a piece of felt just big enough to cover the felt ball will keep the bag closed. Felt balls can also be used to conceal the place where a braid has been sewn onto a bag and add more decoration. A number of different-coloured felt balls sewn onto a hat, either in a cluster or spaced out, can look very effective. When making a jacket, felt balls can be used to make fastenings instead of buttons. If the felt balls are cut in half and the flat surface placed onto the item and secured with embroidery stitches the semi-circle of felt will make an interesting decoration. In fact, felt balls can be used to decorate anything from bags to slippers, mittens to cushions.

Insects and flowers can also be used to decorate felt garments, eg add a bumble bee or two to a pair of slippers or mittens, or cover a jacket with felt flowers. Insects and flowers also look good sewn onto hats and bags.

Fruits can also be used in the same way on garments and there is no reason why you shouldn't use them on a wallhanging. Using all types of felt decorations can add that special finishing touch to any item made from felt.

8
BAGS, HATS, SLIPPERS AND MITTENS

Once you have mastered the art of creating your
own unique fabrics by whatever technique of
felt making suits you, it is time to decide
what to make.

Before you start to make the felt you will need to consider the design and texture of the felt which has to be suitable for the item you intend to make.

The question you may ask yourself is 'Where do I start?'. Start by looking at all the samples of felt you have produced. By studying the felt you have made you can decide what it is you like and dislike in each piece.

COLOUR AND TEXTURE

It is possible you may decide you prefer using natural-coloured fleece and therefore produce felt of natural colours or one colour. The colours of natural fleece vary from white to black and cream to brown so you have plenty of choice. Alternatively, you may prefer using only dyed fleece.

Another important consideration is the texture of the felt. Decide which of your samples was most successful for thickness, firmness and surface appearance. The type of fleece you use will affect the overall texture and feel of the felt. Keep notes of the fleece or mixture of fibres you like the most. The thickness of the felt will depend on what you are going to use it for.

PATTERN

Finally, you need to consider the surface pattern of the felt. You may want to make a perfectly plain piece of felt and then decorate it with machine or hand embroidery. If you prefer patterned felt the design can be made with coloured fleece, yarn or lace. When deciding whether to make a pattern or leave the felt plain, bear in mind how the pattern will look on the item you want to make. A large pattern often looks better on a larger item. Small objects are better with small patterns.

You have two options when thinking about designs and what to make. You can either produce a piece of felt and then decide what to make with it. Or you can decide what article you want to make and then make the felt suitable for that object. Sometimes you may find a piece of felt lends itself to being made into a particular garment or accessory. Usually it is easier to decide what you want to make and then design the felt.

STARTING A PROJECT

A good way to start is to set yourself a project. This project should be set within your capabilities, that is, not too large and complicated that it becomes a problem rather than a pleasure. Think about what you would like to make for yourself, your home or a friend. If you decide to make something for yourself it could be something to wear such as a hat or waistcoat. A decoration for your home in the form of a wall-hanging, chair cover or mobile will be admired and commented on. You might decide to make a gift for someone such as a toy, a pair of mittens or a bag.

When you have decided what the finished article will be you can start to think about the felt design. This could be as straightforward as repeating one of the samples you liked, but make it on a larger scale, or you could give your project a theme. The theme of your project can be based on a particular like or interest of your own, or the colour scheme of a room, or to the particular taste of a friend. By deciding on a theme you have given yourself a starting point for finding inspiration.

GAINING INSPIRATION

There are lots of ways to gain inspiration for your felt designs. If you have decided on a theme it may help to study photographs in books or visit exhibitions of paintings, museums and art galleries. Alternatively you may have things around you at home that you like the pattern of. The pattern in a carpet or jumper may give you the inspiration you need for colour and shape. There are of course lots of interesting shapes and colours and patterns outside the home. You may be inspired by a visit to a local beauty spot or a visit to a town or city with interesting architecture.

At this stage it helps to have a sketch book or piece of paper to draw on. When you have decided what you are going to make you will need to make a pattern for the final product. The paper pattern can be a commercial one, copied from another object or made by yourself using the diagrams in this chapter. When the pattern has been made for your design you can then think about the type of felt you will need to make and how much of it.

If you decide to make a plain felt then the felt design is quite straightforward. If you want to make a piece of felt from coloured fleece you will need to choose your colours. It is worth taking time over this choice. The colours you choose may be from a painting, photograph, an outfit or a room. To help you decide what colours to use it helps to experiment with paints, crayons, woollen yarn or fleece. By mixing different colours together you will arrive at a particular colour combination you like. Then the fleece you are going to use can be dyed in these colours.

You may then make the final decision – the surface design. You may want the texture of the fleece to produce the design or you may want to pattern the surface with yarn, lace or shaped coloured fleece. This

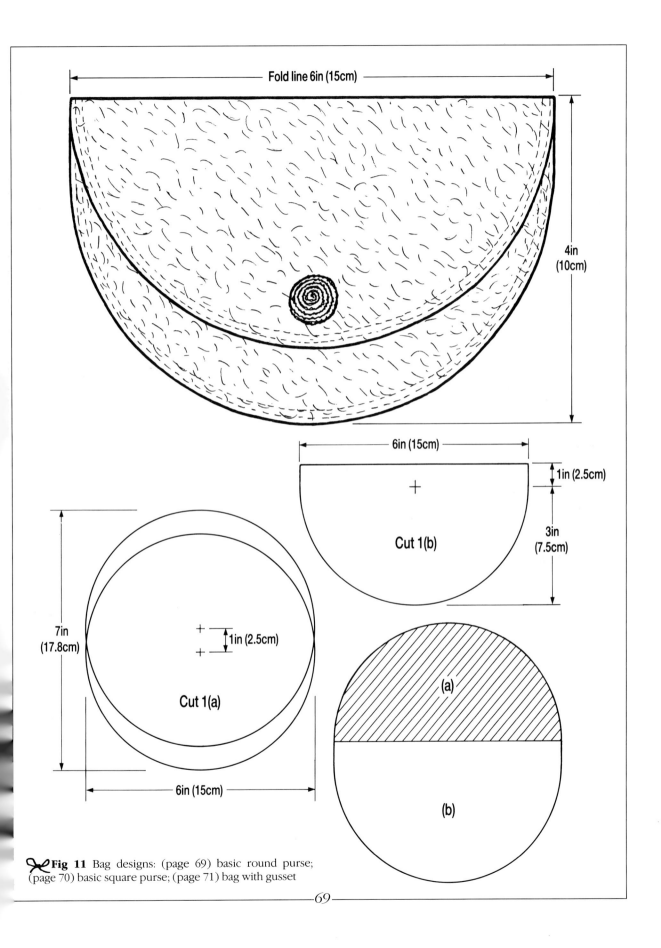

Fold line 6in (15cm)

4in (10cm)

6in (15cm)

1in (2.5cm)

Cut 1(b)

3in (7.5cm)

7in (17.8cm)

1in (2.5cm)

Cut 1(a)

6in (15cm)

(a)

(b)

Fig 11 Bag designs: (page 69) basic round purse; (page 70) basic square purse; (page 71) bag with gusset

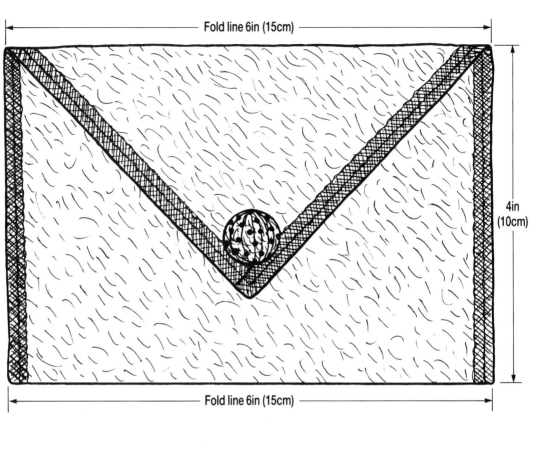

Fold line 6in (15cm)

4in
(10cm)

Fold line 6in (15cm)

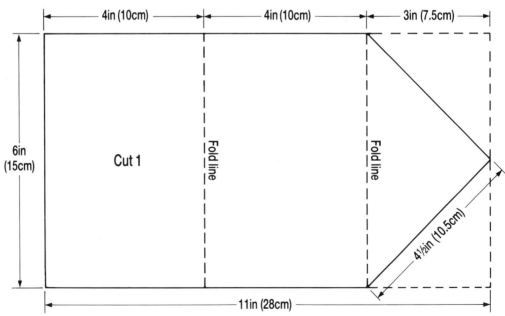

4in (10cm)

4in (10cm)

3in (7.5cm)

6in
(15cm)

Cut 1

Fold line

Fold line

4½in (10.5cm)

11in (28cm)

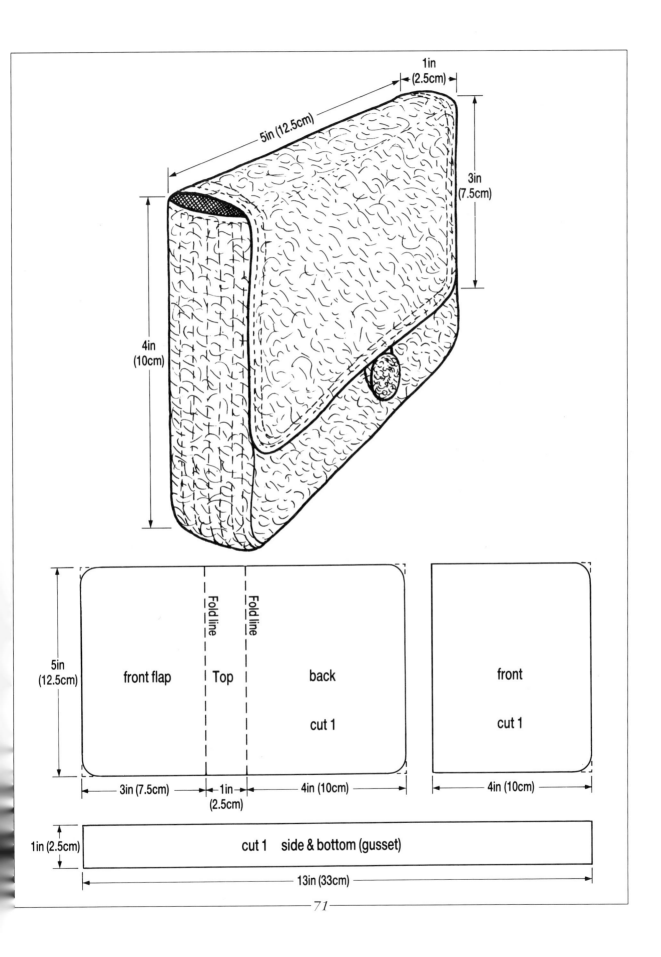

1in
(2.5cm)

5in (12.5cm)

3in
(7.5cm)

4in
(10cm)

5in
(12.5cm)

Fold line

Fold line

front flap

Top

back

cut 1

front

cut 1

3in (7.5cm)

1in
(2.5cm)

4in (10cm)

4in (10cm)

1in (2.5cm)

cut 1   side & bottom (gusset)

13in (33cm)

surface pattern could be a repeated design or an over-all picture with no repeat. The size of the pattern on the felt will depend on the dimensions of the finished article.

If you have only made sample-size pieces of felt before it is a good idea not to jump straight in and make enormous pieces. The piece of felt you are going to make wants to be large enough for the final product but easy enough to handle. If after making the paper pattern you need a large piece of felt, a good way around this is to make a few smaller pieces. Each piece of the paper pattern can be placed on each piece of the felt.

BAGS

Well-made felt, patterned or plain, is ideal for making bags. The felt has to be well milled and quite firm to make it strong and hard wearing. It is best to avoid felt with a pattern that is likely to pull away. The felt will have to be reasonably strong to carry the weight of the articles placed inside. It can be reinforced with machine stitching or by quilting in a lining.

To decide on the design of the bag you can either copy a favourite bag or buy a pattern (see Fig 11 for designs). Once you have the basic design and the pattern pieces you can work out how much felt you will need, and whether you can make several small pieces or one biggish piece. If the bag design you have chosen consists of several panels, it may be fun to make each panel a different colour or pattern with the felt.

Take the paper pattern and lay it out flat to see how much felt you will need. When you have made the felt you can place the paper pattern onto the felt and cut out each piece making sure you have enough. Then sew it together by hand or machine and add felt decorations or braids.

MITTENS

Felt mittens are wonderfully warm to wear and are ideal in wintry conditions as they really do insulate against the cold. They also make good presents and are quick and easy to make. Do not use too thick or very coarse fleece, however, as you will want to be able to flex your hands and move your fingers. There-fore a thinnish soft felt is most suitable.

There are three different ways of making mittens. You can make mittens that are sewn together and have seams, using flat felt and a paper pattern or you can make fingerless mittens from the same pattern by cutting off the rounded tip.

Making seamless mittens

If you have tried the sampling method of making a seamless pocket, then making the mittens will not be very difficult. The principles are basically the same. It is just the shape that is slightly more complex and therefore a bit more care is necessary.

METHOD

1 Start by making a pattern. This can be made from your own hand or from the hand of the person it is intended for. Place the hand onto a piece of paper. Let the fingers relax so that they are not close together or wide apart. The thumb should be angled out away from the hand. Now keep the palm flat on the paper and with a pencil draw a line around the shape of the hand and thumb leaving a gap of approximately 2.5cm (1in). The gap between your hand and the line you draw will allow for the felted seam and shrinkage in the felt-making process.

When you have made the pattern of your hand, then cut out the shape. You now need to transfer the mitten pattern onto a sheet of polythene. A plastic bag will be suitable but it must not have any holes in it and must be strong enough to survive the felt-making proce-dure. Place the paper pattern of your hand onto the polythene and cut out two identical shapes, one for each hand. The plastic template forms the structure of the mitten and is therefore very important. You may find it helps you at the next stage if you outline the plastic template with black felt-tip pen. Otherwise you may not be sure where the edge of the template is.

2 Once the pattern has been made you will need to card the fleece and make it up into carded layers. Obviously with a pair of mittens you have an inside and an outside. Therefore you can make them in different colours and patterns. For each mitten you will need two pieces of carded felt layers (see Plate 33). Take one of the carded layers of fleece (about four layers will be thick enough) and place the plastic template on it. The edge of the mitten pattern where your hand enters the mitten needs to come off the edge of the carded fleece. With a few pins secure the template to the carded fleece. Then take your scissors and cut around the template leaving a gap of about 2cm (3/4in) between the pattern and the cut edge.

3 Sew the polythene template into the fleece but leave the opening edge free. Start by turning back the allowance onto the plastic pattern. Do this all the way around the shape. Take more care around the thumb to make sure you keep the fleece smooth and even. Turn back the fleece and pin as you go (see Plate 34). When all the turning allowance has been turned and pinned back you will need to tack it into place and then remove all the pins. This will leave the plastic

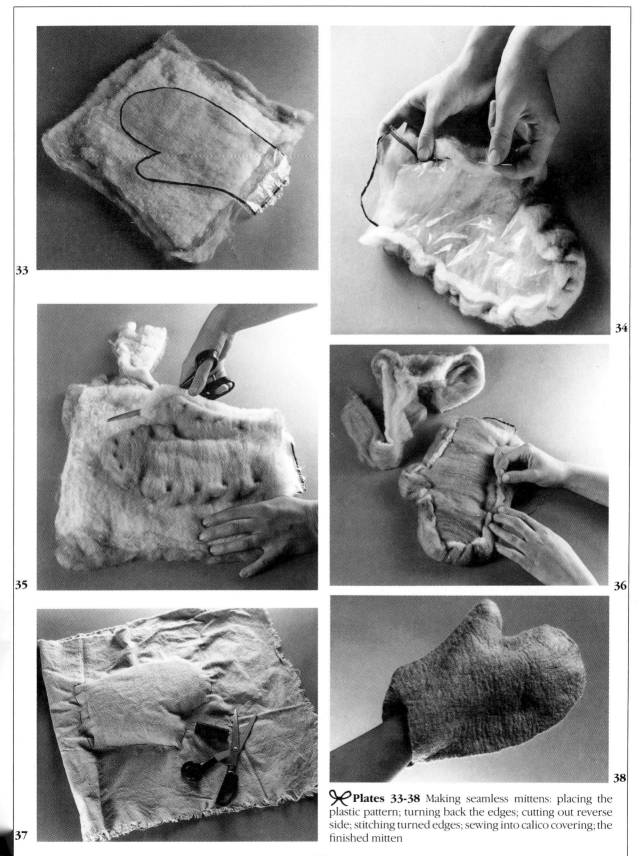

33

34

35

36

37

38

✂ **Plates 33-38** Making seamless mittens: placing the plastic pattern; turning back the edges; cutting out reverse side; stitching turned edges; sewing into calico covering; the finished mitten

73

template trapped in the fleece but leaving the opening edge free and not covered by fleece.

✂ 4 The next stage is to place the other side of the mitten on top of the first piece. The format is more or less the same as step 3. Take the second piece of carded fleece layers and place the half mitten with template sewn in onto the carded fleece. At this stage you can decide which way you want the fleece to run. The carded fleece lays in parallel lines. Therefore the fleece can run from side to side on both sides of the mitten or from top to bottom. Alternatively, you could make the fleece run in a different direction on either side. Remember to make the second mitten in the same way as the first one but in mirror image.

When you have decided which way the fleece is going to run, place the half mitten onto the fleece. Keep the open edge to the edge of the carded fleece. Pin the half mitten into place and then cut around the shape leaving a gap of 2cm (¾in) for turning (see Plate 35). Once the other half of the mitten has been cut out all the edges except the open edge can be turned back and pinned, then finally tacked into place (Plate 36). At this stage you should be able to place your finger tips inside the un-felted mitten through the open edge. Make sure that the turned edges are neat and keep the shape of the mitten particularly around the thumb. Check all the pins have been removed.

✂ 5 The mittens now need to be sewn into the cotton covering to protect the fleece during the wet stage. Cover each mitten separately (see Plate 37) with the cotton covering. Then with large tacking stitches, sew through the covering as close as you can to the felt mitten. The calico parcel will look quite puffy but will soon compress at the wet stage.

✂ 6 Follow the hand-felting procedure described in Chapter 3. When you have reached the rolling stage when the cotton covering has been removed, continue to roll with the plastic template still in place. Gradually the mitten will shrink quite considerably. Check the opening in the mittens frequently to make sure it doesn't become felted together. When the felt feels very firm and the mittens have shrunk enough to crinkle the template, the tacking stitches should be removed and the plastic template pulled out gently from inside the mittens.

Remove the tacking stitches very carefully and then pull the plastic template out through the open edge of the mittens. If the template is difficult to remove then gently turn the mitten inside out (if the felt is fully milled there will be no problem doing this). When the tacking stitches and the template have been removed you can place your hand inside the mitten and make sure the thumb is open inside. At this point if the mitten is still much larger than your hand you can make it fit better by continuing to roll the felt. During the final rolling stage keep placing your hand inside the mitten to stop the two sides from felting together.

When the rolling stage is complete the mittens can be pinned onto a board and left to dry. Once the mittens are dry you can decide whether to cut the open edges or to leave the natural felted opening. The mittens can be decorated or left plain. Either way you will have a pair of extremely warm mittens with no seams.

Making mittens with seams

An easier way to make felt mittens is to make them from one piece of felt with seams. Ideally you want to have the minimum of seams possible, as the fewer there are the easier the mittens are to make and the less bulky they look. The seam around the thumb wants to be as small as possible. The deep curve between the thumb and the hand will need to be snipped along the seam allowance down to the sewing line. This will make the mitten fit more comfortably.

MAKING THE PATTERN

Start by making the pattern to fit your hand before you make the felt. Once you have made the pattern you will know how large the pieces of felt will need to be. To make the pattern, place your hand palm downwards onto a piece of paper. Keep the fingers relaxed and angle the thumb outwards. Draw around your hand, leaving a gap of 2.5cm (1in) between the hand and the drawn line. The open edge of the mitten can finish on the wristbone or higher. You now have the basic pattern.

CUTTING OUT

From the basic pattern you will need to cut out four pieces of felt (two pieces for each hand). Take care when cutting the felt to make sure you have cut the felt for a left and right hand. This is very important if you are using different patterned pieces of felt for each side and you want each mitten to be identical.

SEWING TOGETHER

When you come to sew the mittens together you will have one seam that follows the shape of the hand. The mitten can be sewn together with the seam on the inside or the outside. If you decide to have the seam inside the mitten it is easier to use a plain open seam and snip the curve between the thumb and the hand. If you make the seam on the outside of the mitten a feature can be made of the multicoloured layers of fleece. The outside seam could be finished with hand embroidery to produce a scalloped edge or machine stitching to make a stiff neat flat edge. An outside seam will probably need to be trimmed for a neat shape.

Mittens made from one piece of felt

Instead of having one seam to join the two pieces of mitten together, a pattern can be made so that you only need to cut two pieces of felt for a pair of mittens. You can adapt the basic pattern to make the new pattern. To do this place the basic paper pattern onto another piece of paper and draw around the shape. Now turn the pattern over and place it flush to the shape you have just drawn with the thumbs together. Draw around the paper pattern again and then remove it. You will be left with another pattern of a mitten in mirror image from the thumb. If you use this pattern for your mittens you will need large pieces of felt. The advantage is that you will not need to make a seam along the thumb as this is where the felt will be folded.

An alternative to this mitten pattern can be made by placing the fold line on the outside of the hand. The seam will go from the tip of the little finger around the rest of the hand and thumb up to the wrist. If you use this pattern for your mittens you will have to use an inside seam to produce a neat shape.

By using the basic pattern as a guide, a variety of different shaped mittens can be made. The shape can be exaggerated at the wrist to make an arrowhead or semi-circular shape. The inside of the wrist can be cut shorter than the outside. Very easily fingerless mittens can be made by cutting the pattern across where the tips of the fingers would be. Always make a paper pattern first and try this on your hand before cutting out the felt.

When finishing off the mittens the raw edges can be covered with bias strips of material or turned and stitched down. For added decoration the flat felt shape of the mittens could be quilted with machine stitching before being sewn together.

SLIPPERS

Another fun and relatively easy small item to make from felt is slippers. They are comfortable and warm to wear and will last fairly well if worn only indoors. The slipper needs to fit quite well and the felt needs to be well made and strong as there are more pressure points and places where the felt will rub.

You can make two types of slippers from felt – either slippers made in one piece with no seams or slippers cut from a flat pattern. With either type there are lots of variations that can be made from the basic pattern.

Making seamless slippers

The procedure for making slippers in one piece with no seams is very similar to making pockets or mittens with no seams. The difference lies in the finishing off.

MAKING THE PATTERN

First, you need to make a pattern which should be made into a plastic template. The size of the pattern is based on the foot measurement of the person the slippers are intended for. Place the foot onto a piece of paper and draw a line to show the total length of the foot. To find the depth of the foot, take a tape measure and measure the width across the foot at the broadest point, the base of the toe joints. On the paper mark this measurement up from the first drawn line. Next, measure the ankle depth by measuring from the ankle to the side of the foot and mark this on the paper. Then measure the width of the ankle and mark this on the paper. The points give you the outline of your pattern. Now you can join up these points to make the shape of the slipper. The pattern will look more like a sock. Draw another line outside the pattern leaving a gap of 2.5cm (1in). This will allow for the pattern to cover half the foot. To check that the pattern fits, cut out the paper pattern and try against the inside of the foot. It should cover half the foot from the middle of the sole of the foot to halfway across the instep.

The slipper will be made up of two pieces based on this shape. Therefore the paper pattern needs to fit quite well. When you are satisfied with your slipper pattern it can be transferred onto polythene to make two templates outlined in black felt-tip pen (see photographs).

METHOD

1 You will need four pieces of carded fleece about four layers thick and large enough for the polythene template and a turning allowance. Remember when carding the fleece to note which way the fibres are lying as you will have the inside and outside to consider. Therefore the colour and pattern can be different on either side. Place the plastic template onto the carded fleece with the open ankle edge on the edge of the carded layers. Pin the template to the fleece and cut around the shape leaving a gap of 2.5cm (1in). This will allow for turning and shrinkage (see Plate 39).

2 With the template pinned into place fold back the turning allowance onto the plastic template. Pin the turned fleece into place all the way round except for the ankle opening and then tack and remove pins (see Plate 40).

3 Now place this onto another piece of carded fleece and cut out the other side of the slipper leaving

✂ **Plates 39-44** Making seamless slippers: cutting around plastic pattern; turning back the edges; cutting out reverse side; stitching down the turned edges; unfelted boot; felted slipper

a turning allowance of 2.5cm (1in) (see Plate 41). Fold back the allowance and pin and then tack into place. The unmade boot will have the template sewn into place and you should be able to place your fingers through the ankle opening (see Plate 43).

✂4 When the carded fleece has been stitched around the template cover the unmade slipper with the cotton sheet. Then stitch the shape into the cotton covering by stitching through the cotton close to the slipper. Now follow the hand-felting method in Chapter 3. After the cotton covering has been removed continue rolling the slipper until the felt has shrunk considerably. Only when the felt is well made and fully shrunk can you remove the plastic template. This can be done most successfully by turning the slipper inside out and removing all tacking stitches and the plastic. Continue rolling until it fits.

✂5 The finished slipper will look more like a sock (see Plate 44) and forms the basic shape of the slipper. After the slippers are dry they can be decorated (see Colour Plate 15). When deciding how to finish and decorate the slippers, it helps to place them on the foot. This will flatten out the whole of the slipper and you may need to cut the opening. Add felt-ball decorations and hand embroidery to give strength. To make the slippers extra hard-wearing a leather sole can be sewn on.

There are a variety of designs that can be made from this one method. It depends on how you decide to finish off the slippers and if you decide to cut away some of the felt or leave it like a boot. If the slipper is left to look like a boot, ribbons can be used to suggest lacing and the top could be rolled down to show the inside. Consider all the possibilities before cutting the felt slipper.

Making slippers from a flat pattern

It is far easier to make slippers from a flat pattern. The various pieces that make up the slippers will need to be sewn together and therefore there will be a few seams. Once the basic pattern has been made for a pair of slippers it can be altered and added to giving a variety of different shapes (see Fig 12).

It always helps to base the size and shape of the pattern on the foot it is intended for. That way you can always check that the pattern is going to fit before you cut the felt. By making a pair of slippers from a flat pattern you can use a combination of different types and patterns of felt.

The basic flat pattern consists of the sole of the slipper, the heel and the toe piece. All you need to do to make the sole is to draw around the shape of the foot with the sole of the foot flat on a sheet of paper. Keep the pencil at a 90° angle to the paper as you move

it around the foot. This will ensure you have the exact shape of the foot.

To make the heel of the slipper you will need a piece of paper long enough to go around half of the foot, that is, halfway between the toes and the heel on one side to the same point on the other side of the foot. The height of the heel piece is dictated by the height of the ankle bone. When placing the paper around the foot you can decide how deep you want the slipper to be.

To make the toe pattern you need to place a piece of paper across the front of the foot to cover the toes up to the side of the foot. The heel pattern joins the toe pattern on each side. This is how you decide where the toe pattern starts. The shape across the top of the toe piece can be cut flat or curved. When the paper is in place across the toes, smooth the paper over the foot and draw a line around the toes next to the sole of the foot. This will make the front part of the slipper.

When you have cut out each piece of the paper pattern, place the pieces around the foot to see how they fit. Make sure the side seams will be equal on each side. When you are satisfied with the pattern you can make an identical copy so that you have six pieces of paper pattern. These can now be placed onto the felt you are going to use. Before cutting out the felt make sure you can leave a seam allowance of 3cm (½in) and you will have a left and right foot.

TO MAKE UP THE SLIPPERS

To add strength to the slippers each piece can be machine embroidered and quilted and a lining can be added at this stage if desired. Start by joining the side seam of the toe piece and heel. Use either a plain flat open seam or a french enclosed seam to hide the raw edges. A flat seam can either be hidden inside the slipper or made a feature of on the outside.

The next stage is to sew the upper pieces to the sole of the slippers. To do this, mark the centre back of the heel and the centre front of the toe with a pin. Now place on top of the sole and pin all the way round. The side seams should be parallel on each side of the foot. Once you have positioned the pieces correctly the two can be sewn together. The seam can be either inside the slipper or outside. For a hidden seam you will need to place the pieces with the right sides together and then turn the slippers out the right way. To make a feature of the join on the outside, you can pin the upper straight onto the sole and stitch into place. This will be particularly interesting if the felt is made from multicoloured layers.

It is a good idea to use machine stitching to sew the pieces together. This will make the slippers much stronger. Once they have been sewn together the

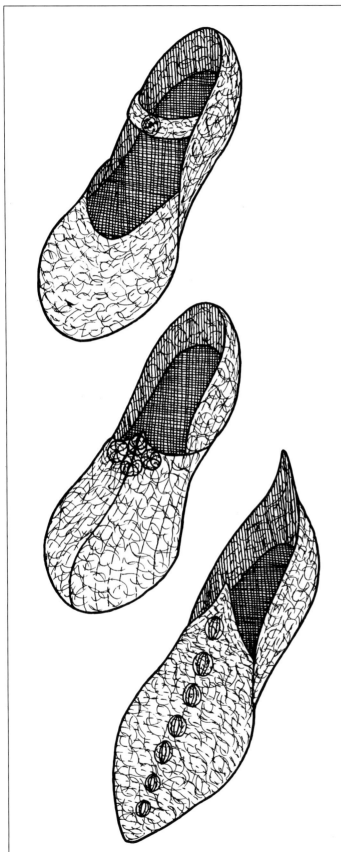

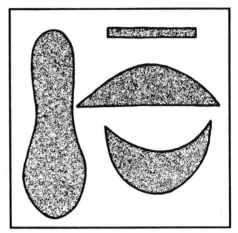

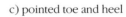

✂ **Fig 12** Slippers cut from flàt pattern:
a) rounded front with bar strap;

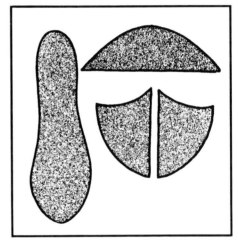

b) high at front with central seam;

c) pointed toe and heel

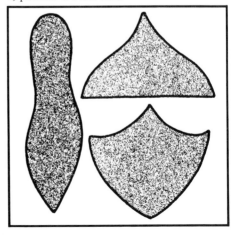

slipper should be tried on to see how they fit and how easy they are to put on and take off. Also at this stage you can decide whether to add straps or ties to keep the slippers on. Edges can be trimmed with braids, bias-binding or machine or hand embroidery. For extra hard wear a leather sole should be added. If you want to add a leather sole this is easier to do before you assemble the whole slipper.

Once the slippers have been sewn together and fitted, any additional decorations such as felt balls, insects or flowers can be added.

The patterns can be adapted by exaggerating the basic shape, eg the heel can be made higher at the back or the front of the slipper can be made pointed. By making a variety of patterns from the basic design you will have lots of ideas to choose from.

HATS

Felt naturally lends itself to hat making as it is relatively easy to mould into a shape to fit the head. Alternatively, the shape of a hat can be made from a flat pattern. The good thing about making hats is that you do not need to have sophisticated equipment, just a little patience and imagination. If you have not made hats before, start with a simple design before making something complicated. If your first attempts do not turn out how you expected they can still be used to make interesting shapes.

How to block a hat

To block a simple hat made on a mould you need very little equipment. The mould will dictate the shape of your hat and needs to be made of something that can be pinned into and won't be harmed by water and heat. An ideal form to block a hat on is a wooden hat block or, failing that, a polystyrene wig stand. (Your local hairdresser may be able to help.)

If you have not blocked or moulded a hat on a head shape before then try something very simple. The most simple blocked shape is a skull cap. To block the skull cap you will need a rounded head shape (a wig stand or hat block) made from wood or polystyrene and a piece of felt approximately 25.5cm (10in) square.

To shape the felt into a skull cap, you will need to soak the felt in hot water until the water has penetrated through the felt. Remove the felt from the water and squeeze out any excess water. Then pull the felt over the head shape, tugging hard on each side equally, pulling the felt down. Felt is very elastic and as long as you have made the felt well it will be strong enough to be pulled and stretched. Gradually the felt will take on the shape of the mould. As the felt begins

to shape it helps to start pinning it to the mould. You can use either dressmaker's pins if your mould is made from polystyrene or drawing pins if the mould is made from wood.

Start by pinning the felt in the centre at the top and then pull the felt down equally on opposite sides. As you pull the felt down, pin it and move your hands around the shape. You should be able to pull hard enough to make sure you do not leave any puckers or creases in the felt. Ideally you want the felt to be as smooth as possible. Once the felt has been fully stretched and pinned to the mould, it then needs to be left to dry. As the felt dries it will shrink and retain the shape of the block. When the felt is dry it can be unpinned. The skull cap will not be a regular shape so you will need to trim it. Use tailor's chalk to draw in the required cutting line. You can either make a feature of points and dips or cut the shape very neatly and symmetrically.

When you have decided where to cut the felt, the excess felt can be cut away and kept on one side. It is worth keeping the felt trimmings as they can be used to decorate the hat.

The basic skull cap is now ready to be finished and trimmed. Machine or hand embroidery can be used or the addition of cut pieces of felt appliquéd to the skull cap. The edges can be covered or turned and stitched. Felt-ball motifs are rather fun to use to decorate hats. The simple skull cap could be turned into an exotic cocktail hat, a child's dressing-up hat or a part of a theatrical costume.

A BLOCKED BRIMMED HAT

An extension of the skull cap is to make a brimmed hat. The moulding procedure is much the same as the skull cap but instead of cutting away the excess, the felt is used to make the brim.

✄ 1 Take a piece of felt approximately 41cm (16in) square. Soak the felt in hot water and then stretch across the mould. As the felt is stretched and pulled down around the mould you need to decide the depth of the crown. Depending on your felt you may be able to get a deep crown or it may have to be quite shallow. It will probably help when you are pulling the felt to stretch a piece of elastic over the felt and the block. If the elastic rests at the deepest point this will mark the depth of the crown. Then you can pin just under the elastic to make a symmetrical crown of even depth. This then needs to be left to dry (see Colour Plate 16).

✄ 2 Once the felt is dry you can work on the brim. With the felt still attached to the block, pull the excess felt outwards to suggest the brim. Make sure there are no puckers under the elastic and gently ease the

Colour Plate 16 A piece of felt being blocked on a head shape

excess felt back towards the elastic to produce a flat brim. To keep the depth of the crown and keep the shape it is a good idea to run a line of tacking stitches where the elastic is. When this has been done the elastic and pins can be removed and the felt taken off the block.

✂3 Now the half-made hat needs to be placed on a flat surface to spread the brim out. The crown will stand up in a dome. Using a steam iron the brim should be pressed up to the line of tacking stitches. The brim is now beginning to take shape. When the brim is flat you can measure from the tacking stitches outwards all the way round to mark the edge of the brim. Draw the edge of the brim with tailor's chalk and then trim away the excess felt.

✂4 The brim will probably be quite floppy because of the weight of the felt, in which case you will need to stiffen the brim. There are several ways you can do this. You can machine stitch with straight stitch, zigzag lots of concentric lines of stitches close together, or wire the edge. Alternatively, a stiffening agent can be used – either diluted PVA or a millinery felt stiffener.

To finish the hat, cover the edges with bias-binding, braids or feathers and maybe add some felt decorations.

To make a very deep crown from felt make a pocket of felt with seams that is large enough to cover the block and your head. The pocket can then be stretched over the block.

There are so many different designs you can produce from these simple blocking techniques. The crown can be made deeper on one side than the other. The brim can be cut in an irregular shape. The use of felt decorations can completely transform a very plain hat into an exotic creation.

Making a hat from a flat pattern

A wide range of hat shapes can be made from a paper pattern. This method wastes less felt and you do not need to use blocks or head shapes.

PILLBOX

The easiest hat that can be made from a flat pattern is the pillbox hat. To make a pillbox you need two pieces of felt for the top and the side. If your pieces of felt are quite small the side can be made up from a number of smaller pieces sewn together. The paper pattern for a pillbox can be made to measure.

HOW TO MAKE A PILLBOX PATTERN

✂1 Measure the head that the hat is intended for at the deepest point where the hat will sit. This measurement forms the basis of the pattern. You need to make a circle or oval with a circumference the same as the head measurement.

$$\text{eg Head size} \quad 58.5\text{cm} (23\text{in}) = 2\pi R$$
$$58.5\text{cm} (23\text{in}) = 6.28 \times R$$
$$R = \frac{58.5\text{cm} (23\text{in})}{6.28} = 9.5\text{cm} (3.66\text{in})$$

This will make the radius of your circle 9.5cm (3.66in). Draw this onto paper and this will make the top pattern for the hat.

✂2 To make the side of the pillbox, cut a strip of paper the same length as the head size and as deep as you need it, eg 58.5cm (23in) x 10cm (4in).

✂3 When you are cutting out the felt leave a seam allowance of 1.3cm (½in). This allows for seams and turning edges.

✂4 To sew the two pieces together, pin the side felt to the top inside out and sew all the way round. Where the side piece overlaps at the back, stitch the seam flat. It can be sewn together by hand or machine.

✂5 The pillbox can be lined or the edges can be turned back to finish it off. The pillbox lends itself very well to decoration.

BERET

The other shape that is very easy to make from a flat pattern is the beret. A basic beret consists of two circles, one has a circle cut out where it fits on to the head. A cuff band can be added to make the beret fit more comfortably.

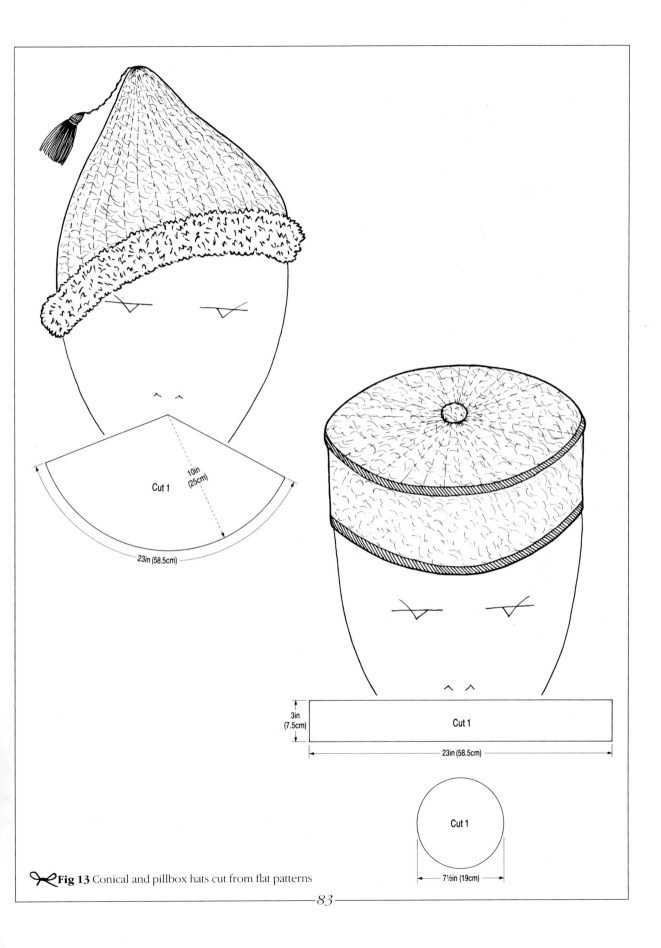

Cut 1

10in
(25cm)

23in (58.5cm)

3in
(7.5cm)

Cut 1

23in (58.5cm)

Cut 1

7½in (19cm)

✄**Fig 13** Conical and pillbox hats cut from flat patterns

TO MAKE THE PATTERN

✂ 1 To make a pattern to fit, first measure the head it is intended for and decide how large you want the hat to be, eg head size 58.5cm (25in); beret size 36cm (14in) diameter. Cut two paper circles with a 18cm (7in) radius.

✂ 2 Take one of the circles and draw another circle the same circumference as the head measurement. Cut the inner circle out and try the pattern on your head.

✂ 3 For the cuff band cut a strip of paper 5cm (2in) deep x the head measurement, eg 5cm (2in) x 58.5cm (25in).

✂ 4 Place the three pieces onto the felt and cut out each piece, leaving a seam allowance of 1.3cm ((½in).

✂ 5 To make up, sew the top circle to the bottom circle with the hole cut out. Turn right side out and press flat.

✂ 6 Join the band of felt to the inside circle and fold the band inwards and stitch down inside the hat.

CONICAL HAT

A very simple and effective hat to make from felt is a conical hat or clown's hat. This can be made from a semi-circle of felt with the outside edge the same as the head measurement. The straight edge makes a seam on the back of the hat. Finish off the edges.

When you have tried making a few hats, you will probably start to design your own patterns. A hat made from a flat pattern may benefit from being blocked as well.

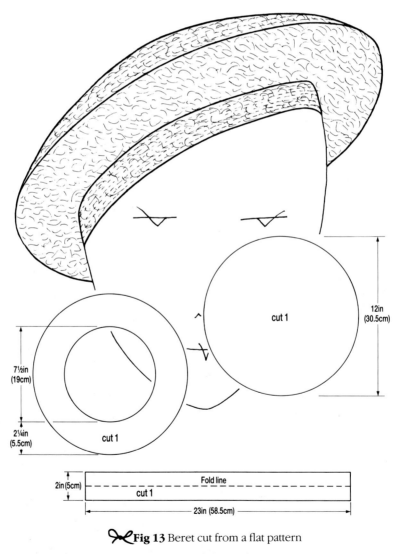

7½in (19cm)

2¼in (5.5cm)

cut 1

cut 1

12in (30.5cm)

2in (5cm) Fold line

cut 1

23in (58.5cm)

✂ **Fig 13** Beret cut from a flat pattern

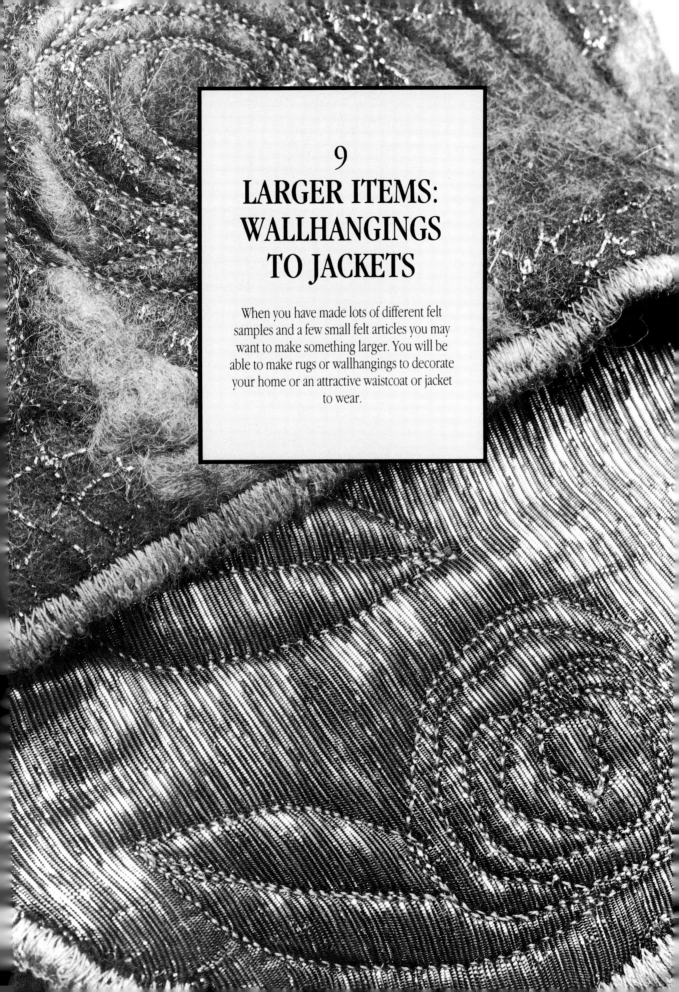

9
LARGER ITEMS: WALLHANGINGS TO JACKETS

When you have made lots of different felt samples and a few small felt articles you may want to make something larger. You will be able to make rugs or wallhangings to decorate your home or an attractive waistcoat or jacket to wear.

To be able to complete larger projects, you will need to make a piece of felt considerably bigger than the pieces you have been making. The larger the piece of felt, the more difficult it will be to handle and therefore you will need to take extra care during the felting process.

The reason a large piece of felt becomes difficult to handle is because of the weight of the fleece. When it has been carded, a large area of fleece is quite difficult to move around. At the carded stage the fleece laid out to make into felt is still very fragile and you want to move it as little as possible. The more the carded fleece is pulled and stretched the more holes and gaps are likely to appear in the final piece of felt. At the wet stage it is particularly important not to move or stretch the fleece. With the added weight of the water it really does need careful handling.

For these reasons when you are making larger pieces of felt you will need slightly different techniques and to find a special place to make it. However, making large areas of felt does not need to be a problem. There are ways of making larger felt items where you do not necessarily have to make one large piece of felt.

EQUIPMENT AND SPACE

If you want to embark on a large piece of felt it is worth planning first where you are going to carry out the wet stage, then, if possible, build up the carded layers in that space.

You will need an area large enough to stamp on the fleece but where you will not get it dirty. This will probably have to be done outside. If you have a paved area in the garden then this will be ideal, or perhaps a garage space can be changed into a felt-making area. The ground can be covered with a large plastic sheet held down with bricks or other heavy articles. The plastic sheet will need to be quite flexible so that you can drain away the cold water.

An alternative to working on the ground is to have a large table. The table will need to be quite sturdy if you intend stamping on the felt. Depending on the surface design you will be able to use an alternative method to harden the felt. A large wooden board that can be made into a table and then placed on the ground is very useful and versatile. This way you can ensure that the fleece is kept flat and undisturbed at every stage.

Once you have decided on a space for making the felt, you will also need a large cotton covering that will cover the carded fleece completely. The cotton sheet must cover the bottom and the top. It is best to place the cotton covering on the table or ground first and then place the carded fleece directly onto the covering. As you build up the carded layers, make sure that you alternate the direction of the fibres each time you start a new layer.

To make a large piece of felt you will need a lot of carded fleece. If you are using a greasy, unprepared fleece, it will need carding particularly well. It will be very laborious to card all the fleece with hand carders, so it may be worth investing in a drum carder, or try and hire one. Some craft suppliers will be able to lend out equipment. Good carding of the fleece makes the felt smooth and makes sure there are no lumps, gaps or holes.

If you do not have access to a drum carder, you may find it easier to use prepared fleece. When laying out the layers you will need to make particularly sure that you place the fleece in even quantities. It is still a good idea to hand card prepared fleece for the top and bottom layers. This will make a more even surface for placing a pattern.

Additional equipment that you may find useful for making large pieces of felt are a wooden mallet, a large cylinder of wood and a cane rolling mat. At the wet stage, you will have quite a large area to pat by hand. Although you may initially have to pat the fleece by hand, once it has been reasonably compressed a wooden mallet will make the patting process a lot easier. If you can get friends or family to help, then you could all work on different areas. Each person will use a varying amount of pressure and energy. Therefore it is best to rotate their positions on the fleece so that the felt gets the same treatment over the whole area. At the stamping stage it will also help to have lots of pairs of feet.

The rolling stage should not be considered until the fleece is quite well compressed. When the fleece is rolled, it will disturb any pattern on the surface of the fleece. If you wait until the fibres are well squashed there will be less movement of the pattern. For a large piece of felt it is helpful to place a cane rolling mat underneath the cotton covering before placing down the carded fleece. It can stay under the fleece during the patting and stamping process. When you start to roll up the fleece, the cane rolling mat will make a very secure background for the fragile carded fleece and also allows the cold water to drain away.

When you reach the rolling stage, it will help enormously to have a smooth cylinder of wood that the covered fleece can be wrapped around. If you are using a cane rolling mat, the fleece and rolling mat can be rolled around the cylinder and then rolled backwards and forwards. The heavier the cylinder of wood, the easier and quicker the rolling process will be. The combination of cane and wood is ideal for retaining the heat of the hot water and letting the cold water drain away. The rolling process can be carried out either on a strong table-top or on the ground. If the rolling is done on the ground you can use your feet to push the fleece backwards and forwards. It may also help to have assistance at this stage. Two or more people can apply a lot of pressure and make the rolling process more efficient.

When making a large piece of felt by the hand-rolling method, it should be treated exactly the same as a small piece. Therefore the cotton covering should not be removed until the fleece is fairly well hardened. Once the cotton covering has been removed, it can be rolled around the wooden cylinder inside the cane mat until it is fully shrunk.

USING THE WASHING MACHINE

You will undoubtedly need more patience when making large pieces of felt but there are ways to make the process a little easier. The hand patting, stamping and rolling method is a good process for a complicated design. With this method you have more control over the felt and the surface pattern, if well stitched into place, is less likely to move around and not attach to the fleece. However, if you do not have a surface design or a pattern that won't spoil if it moves around, then you can use the washing-machine process to harden the felt.

The carded fleece will need to be covered by a cotton covering to make sure none of the fleece is poking out; also it is important that the fleece is never folded against fleece. If this happens, different areas of the felt will felt together. It will be necessary to sew through the covering and through the fleece over the whole area to secure the fleece inside the covering. Then the fleece parcel can be rolled tightly around itself to make a long sausage. The roll will need extra stitches with strong thread to make sure it cannot unravel in the washing machine. This long roll can then be placed in the machine and set on the woollen wash.

On removing from the washing machine the felt should be gently unrolled, then all the tacking stitches removed and the cotton covering gently pulled away. When removing the cotton covering remove one side at a time. Push with one hand on the felt and ease the covering away with the other hand. The felt is unlikely to be properly made at this stage but it will be hardened. Therefore you will need to finish off the milling stage by rolling the felt. The advantage of using the washing machine is that you will have more energy left for rolling the large piece of felt!

If your piece of felt has a complicated design, then you will need to stitch the design into place before covering the fleece. You are better off patting and stamping the fleece first to ensure that your pattern has adhered to the background fleece. When the felt is well hardened, it can be placed in the washing machine, stitched in the cotton covering, to finish off the milling process. As before, it should also be rolled up and secured tightly so that it cannot unravel. Mill on the wool cycle to obtain a well-made piece of felt. On removing from the washing machine you will probably find that the cotton covering will be quite well adhered to the fleece. After removing the tacking stitches, the cotton covering needs to be very carefully pulled away. If the felt is still not firm enough it should be rolled around a woollen cylinder in the usual way to finish it off.

MAKING A LARGE RUG OR WALLHANGING IN A PARTICULAR SHAPE

If you decide to make a large piece of felt intended for use as a rug or wallhanging, then you will need to follow the methods described previously. If your piece of felt is intended for use as a rug it will need to be particularly well made to be able to stand up to the wear and tear it will receive as a floor covering. A wall hanging will also have to be made from a well-felted fleece, otherwise after a while it will begin to sag on the wall.

It is worth considering the best type of fleece to use for this purpose. A rug will be harder wearing if made from a harsher, coarser lower-count fleece, although harder to felt. Therefore it will be worth making a blend of different fleeces. A mix of a soft quick-felting fleece and a coarser one will be quite suitable. The different types of fleece must be well blended at the carding stage otherwise you will end up with areas that have felted and some that have not. A wall hanging can be made from a soft fleece or a mixture as it will not be subjected to the same hard wear as a rug.

When you are making a large piece of felt for a rug or wallhanging there is no reason why it has to be made into a rectangular or square shape. The shape of the rug or hanging could be made more interesting by making it round, oval, diamond or even asymmetrical. To save wasting your fleece by cutting the felt to make the shape, you can lay out the final shape when making up the carded layers.

When you have decided on the overall shape, this needs to be drawn onto the cotton covering as a guideline. Then when you come to place the carded fleece you can lay it inside the drawn shape. As you build up the carded layers, make sure that the edges are kept snipped and neat. When the layers have been finished it may help to trim the edges with scissors, following the drawn line on the cotton covering. Making the edges neat at this stage will mean that you will not have to trim the finished piece of felt. A rug or wallhanging will probably look better with a natural felted edge that is smooth and tapered.

A feature can be made of the edges at the preparation stage. Either a fringe of curly fleece can be inserted into the layers, or an embroidered edge can be made using woollen yarn. Both of these types of edging will felt in during the wet stage. A curly fleece fringe will have to be handled carefully to ensure that it doesn't become twisted and tangled. Therefore it would be better to harden the fleece by hand and foot and then roll in a cane mat rather than place it in the washing machine.

When the rug or wallhanging has been completely felted it may need some extra finishing touches. To hang a large wallhanging successfully, try one of the following methods.

✂1 Make hoops from felt and place in a row along the top edge, then run a pole through the loops and rest the pole on nails in the wall.

✂2 Hidden hanging system. Hand sew a tape onto the top edge at the back of the hanging and thus hide the stitches in the layers of the felt. Then stitch a few curtain rings onto the tape. The rings can be attached to nails on the wall. If the wall hanging does not hang flush with the wall you may need to add a batten of wood at the bottom of the hanging to add weight and help the hanging to lie flat. Alternatively, the hanging could be stretched over a wooden frame and stapled into place.

If you have made a rug and the edges are successfully neat and smooth or fringed with curly fleece, you will not need to add any further finishing detail. If, however, the edges are not neat then you will need to trim them. After trimming the edges you may decide that you want to add some extra detail. Ideally the edges want to be as thin and flat as possible. The thinner the edges, the less likely you are to trip up on the edge of the rug. Therefore it will probably be better to cover the edges with a hard-wearing material like hessian cut into bias strips. To strengthen the rug, it may also help to sew a back covering of hessian onto the reverse side. Remember, the rug may slip around on some floor surfaces so it may be a good idea to place it beside a bed or somewhere away from a main walking area.

MAKING SIMPLE GARMENTS

You may not be interested in making felt for rugs or hangings, but prefer to make felt for garments. You are somewhat limited in your choice of garment because of the structure of the fabric and the drape. If you want to make fitted garments you will find this quite difficult because even thin felt does not hang like material. To make a jacket with a figure-hugging shape you will need to use felt that is very thin with the additional strength of inlaid lace or net.

However, there are various simple garments that can be made from large pieces of felt. It is worth making these before you embark on a waistcoat or jacket. This will not only let you get used to making larger pieces but also allow you to practise finishing of techniques and details. There is no point spending a long time making the felt for a garment if you are not going to finish it off well. The finishing detail will enhance the felt, if well done, but if badly done it will only distract.

Cummerbund

There are a few simple garments you can make that need very little structure and therefore very few, if any, seams. The easiest garment to make is a cummerbund. The size of the cummerbund depends on your waist size and therefore so does the piece of felt. A cummerbund is different from a belt because it does not need a buckle to fasten it. A cummerbund made from felt will not only make an attractive accessory but also a warm and neat garment to cover a waistband.

The piece of felt you will need should be a little larger than your waist measurement and as wide as you want the width of the cummerbund to be: eg for 63.5cm (25in) waist, length of carded fleece will need to be 76cm (30in). This will allow for shrinkage and turning all allowances. The width of the carded fleece will need to be approximately 20.5cm (8in) to allow for shrinkage and shaping.

When the carded fleece is being laid out to these measurements the final design on the top surface can be laid out bearing in mind where the centre of the cummerbund will be. The widest part of the cummerbund will be seen from the front when being worn. Therefore the design in the felt can be laid out with a prominent pattern in the centre and tapering away to the edges (see Fig 14(a)). It will help to make a paper pattern first so that you know how to place the design on the felt. Remember that the felt will shrink so it is a good idea to keep the design to the centre of the felt. Then you will not need to cut away the design when cutting out the cummerbund. The felt that you have to cut away can be kept on one side to make felt decorations or small bags and purses.

Although the piece of felt you need to make for a cummerbund is larger than a sample-size piece of felt,

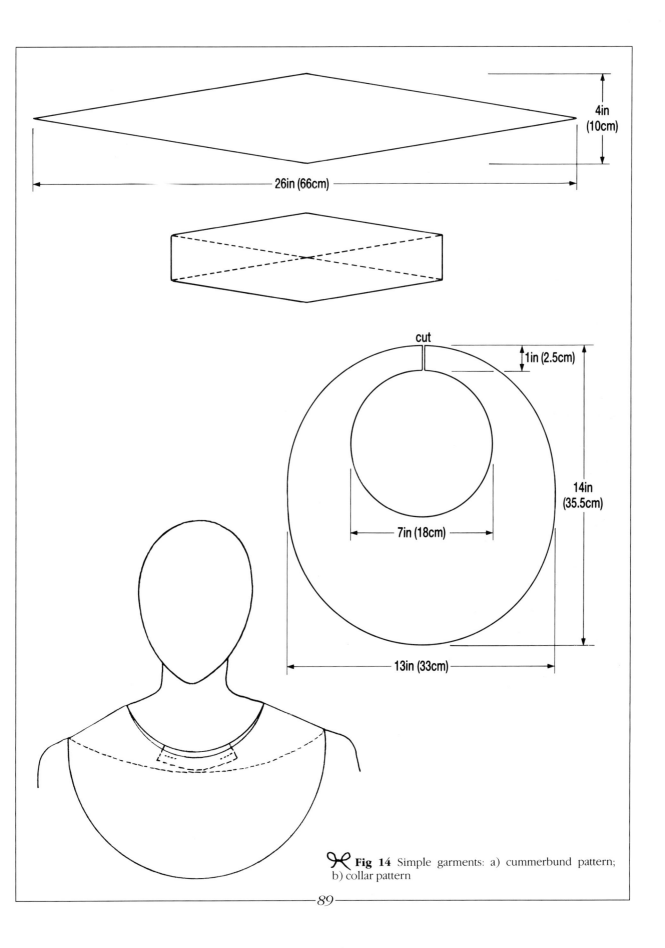

4in
(10cm)

26in (66cm)

cut

1in (2.5cm)

14in
(35.5cm)

7in (18cm)

13in (33cm)

Fig 14 Simple garments: a) cummerbund pattern; b) collar pattern

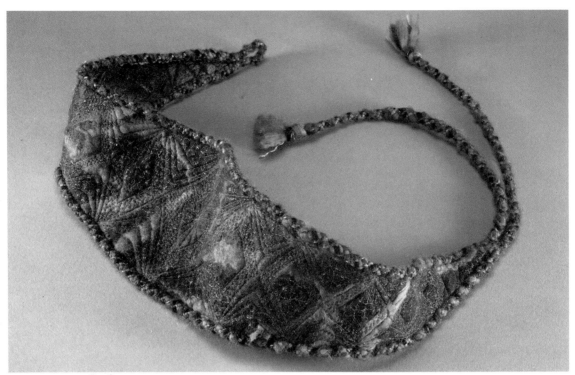

✁**Colour Plates 17 & 18** Simple garments: a cummerbund (above), and collar

it is not too large to be able to make by hand, although you may have to make it in the bath or on a table to be able to find an area large enough to carry out the wet stage.

Once the felt has been made the shape of the cummerbund can be cut out. Place the paper pattern on to the felt, making sure the design on the felt appears in the centre. If you are going to turn the edges you will need to cut a turning allowance. Therefore cut the felt 1.3cm (½in) away from the edge of the paper pattern. If you are going to trim the edges with braid or bias binding, then you can cut the felt flush to the paper pattern.

When the cummerbund has been cut out try it on to see how it fits. One of the advantages of making a felt cummerbund is that the felt can be eased and stretched on one edge to exaggerate the curve of the waistline. To do this use a steam iron and as the iron passes over the felt pull that side to stretch the edges. If this is done all the way along one edge it will give the cummerbund a gentle curved shape and it will fit the body better. All you need to do now is to finish off the garment and decide what fastening to use. The fastenings could be made from felt buttons made from strips of offcut felt or felt balls or braids (see Chapter 10 for ideas). Once you have a basic cummerbund pattern it can be adapted to make lots of different shapes.

A collar

Another simple but effective garment to make is a collar. A felt collar can be made to be worn over a jumper, dress or shirt so it is a very versatile garment. The size of the collar depends on the widths of your shoulders and therefore the size of the piece of felt you need to make is controlled by that measurement.

The shape of felt you will need to make will be a square to allow for the width of the shoulders and the depth back and front: eg for a shoulder width of 38cm (15in), width of carded fleece should be 51cm (20in) by 51cm (20in). This will allow for shrinkage when making the felt and/or trimming the edges.

When you come to decorate the collar it is quite similar to decorating the felt for the cummerbund because you have to consider where the pattern will be on the finished article. Make a paper pattern first (see Fig 14(b)). You will need to cut away a fairly large circle to fit the collar around the neck. Therefore there is no point placing the pattern in the felt at the centre point unless you are going to use it to make something else.

When the felt has been made the shape of the collar can be cut out and tried on. The fastenings can be placed where the opening of the collar overlaps at the back. It is a good idea to make a feature of the fasten-ings and the edges can be finished off to suit the style of the collar and the type of felt you have made (see Chapter 10 for ideas).

MAKING A WAISTCOAT

To make felt for a waistcoat you are going to need considerably more felt than you need for a cummerbund and collar, but this doesn't need to be difficult. You can either make one large piece of felt and then cut it up into the different sections of the waistcoat or you can make a piece of felt for each section. If you decide to make one large piece of felt that will be cut up you will have to consider the overall pattern and where it will appear on the garment. If you want to use patterned felt, the design will have to be fairly uniform but not necessarily in repeat. When each section of the waistcoat is cut out and fitted together the garment will look better if the pattern on the felt covers the whole garment.

If on the other hand each section of the waistcoat is made from a separate piece of felt, then each panel can be made with a separate design. The individual designs can be made to link together when the waistcoat is made up. By making a separate piece of felt for each section the pattern in the felt can be placed exactly where you want the design to appear. For example, you can make the borders of flowers on the shoulders. Another advantage is that the three pieces of felt can all be made at the same time, from carding through to the felting stage. At the wet stage you will be able to save time and energy by stamping on three pieces at once.

Before you start making the felt for the waistcoat you will need to make a paper pattern (see Fig 15). The paper pattern will show you how much felt you will need to make. When you are laying out the carded fleece for each section, allow at least 10cm (4in) all the way around the paper pattern. This will allow for shrinkage and seam allowances. The back section of the waistcoat will be the largest piece of felt and will measure approximately 61cm (24in) x 61cm (24in) depending on the size of the person it is intended for. A piece of felt this size can either be felted by hand or made in the washing machine, the surface design on the felt determining which method to use. Remember the more detailed the design on the felt the flatter it should be kept whilst hardening. Once the felt has been made the paper pattern can be laid onto each panel of felt and the shape cut out leaving a seam allowance of 1.3cm (½in).

To finish off, the waistcoat needs to be sewn together and the raw edges neatened, covered or turned (see Chapter 10). You will also need to decide

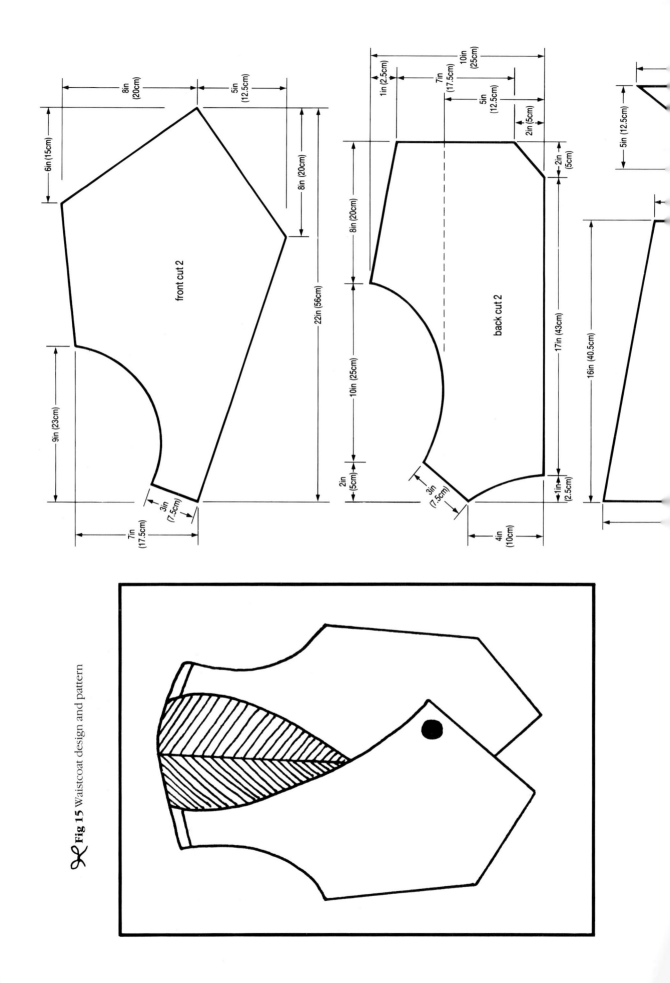

Fig 15 Waistcoat design and pattern

front cut 2

8in (20cm)

5in (12.5cm)

6in (15cm)

8in (20cm)

22in (56cm)

9in (23cm)

3in (7.5cm)

7in (17.5cm)

back cut 2

1in (2.5cm)

7in (17.5cm)

10in (25cm)

5in (12.5cm)

2in (5cm)

2in (5cm)

8in (20cm)

10in (25cm)

17in (43cm)

16in (40.5cm)

2in (5cm)

3in (7.5cm)

1in (2.5cm)

4in (10cm)

5in (12.5cm)

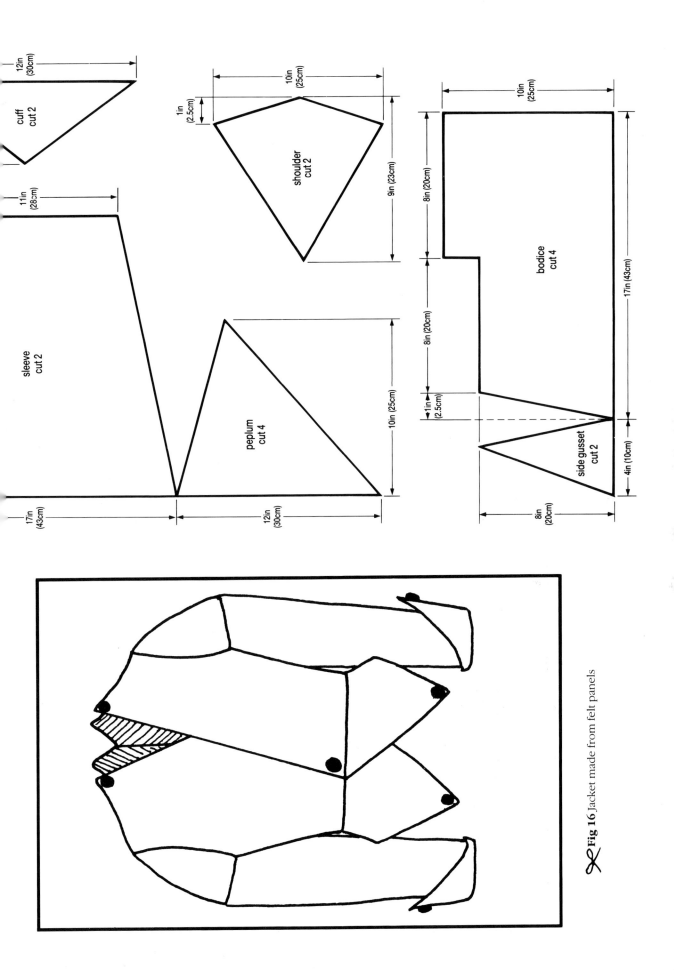

cuff
cut 2

12in
(30cm)

11in
(28cm)

sleeve
cut 2

17in
(43cm)

12in
(30cm)

peplum
cut 4

10in (25cm)

shoulder
cut 2

10in
(25cm)

1in
(2.5cm)

9in (23cm)

bodice
cut 4

10in
(25cm)

8in (20cm)

8in (20cm)

1in
(2.5cm)

side gusset
cut 2

17in (43cm)

4in (10cm)

8in
(20cm)

Fig 16 Jacket made from felt panels

what type of fastenings are needed to keep the waistcoat done up.

A waistcoat made from felt is both attractive and beautifully warm to wear. You may want to line it with contrasting material, or, alternatively, you could try the following technique.

Felting in a lining in a waistcoat

Instead of having to line a waistcoat after you have made the felt the lining could be made to be a part of the felt. The advantage of felting in a lining is that it makes the felt process much easier because you can handle the carded fleece much better. The technique is the same as making felt inlaid with lace net or material.

It is important to choose a material that is fairly thin and which has an open weave so that the wool fibres can travel through the material. A suitable material to use would be a silk georgette or crepe. A polyester equivalent will also work quite well. Avoid any shiny, slippery materials.

METHOD

🎀1 Cut out the paper pattern for the waistcoat. Place the paper pattern onto the lining material. Pin the pattern in place and then cut out the material leaving a margin of at least 10cm (4in) between the pattern and the cutting line. This will allow for shrinkage during the felt-making process. It isn't only the felt that will shrink. The lining will shrink with the wool fibres.

🎀2 Make up the carded layers of fleece for each section of the waistcoat. Make each section a little larger than the lining sections. Place the lining material onto the carded fleece. Cut the carded fleece to the shape of the lining material but leave a 5cm (2in) allowance around the shape.

🎀3 When the lining material is in place on the fleece it is necessary to cut slits approximately 2.5cm (1in) long at 5cm (2in) intervals up and down the lining. Then over the lines of slits place a thin strip of carded fleece (see Plate 46). By doing this you are helping the fleece to attach itself through the lining. Now with tacking stitches sew all the way around the lining material and up and down the line of slits covered with fleece. Do this on each section of the waistcoat so that the lining is securely stitched to the fleece.

🎀4 When the lining has been sewn onto the carded fleece and the slit cut and covered, the carded fleece can be gently turned over. On the other side of the fleece a surface design can be added to each section (see Plate 47). If you are adding a distinctive pattern try and place the motif evenly over the carded fleece. Make sure that any motifs used will not appear unbalanced on the finished garment. You do not want flowers on one side of the waistcoat and none on the other side.

🎀5 When the decoration has been added to the surface of the carded fleece this will need to be stitched with large tacking stitches. The unmade felt will be quite secure because it will be sewn to the lining material.

🎀6 Each section of the waistcoat now needs to be sewn into a cotton covering to protect the pattern and

Plates 45-47 Felting in a lining: carded layers of fleeces; placing in the lining and cutting fleece to shape; showing the cuts and patterned side with half-made felt

Plate 48 Waistcoat – felted panel

lining at the wet stage. Each piece should be covered individually and the stitches should follow the shape of the panel as you sew through the covering.

✂7 Follow the hand-felting method placing the three sections one on top of each other. When they have been well compressed by hand you can continue stamping or place in the washing machine.

✂8 Remove the cotton covering when the felt is well hardened and continue to roll each piece of felt with the lining felted in. The rolling process will make the felt shrink even more and the fibres will travel through the lining. Keep rolling until the felt is very firm.

✂9 Once the felt has been made the tacking stitches can be removed. The felt and lining will now be one piece of felt. Before drying each section of felt check the paper pattern against each piece. Make sure that the lining covers the area that is to be cut out to make the waistcoat. If it has shrunk too much pull the felt into shape and pin flat to dry.

✂10 When the felt is dry the waistcoat is ready to be made up. You will have a waistcoat with a pattern on one side and a felting in lining on the other. All that is left to do is finish the raw edges and add some fastenings (see Chapter 10 for finishing ideas).

JACKET MADE IN PANELS

To make enough felt for a jacket or coat you obviously need far more felt than a waistcoat. In fact, with the addition of the sleeves, you probably need about twice as much felt. Again like the waistcoat you have the choice of making one big piece of felt which is difficult to handle or you can make lots of felt panels that fit together to make the jacket. If you are not used to handling large pieces of felt it is better to make the jacket from panels. For the control that you need you are better off making several pieces to be sewn together.

Making a jacket from panels of felt can often be more interesting than using one large piece. Also, it enables you to add to the shape of the garment as you are making it. When you have worked out the basic pattern for a jacket you can adapt it to make lots of different designs. The basic jacket consists of six panels, two for the back, two for the front and two for the sleeves. The sleeves are the most difficult part to make out of felt as the garment has to be able to move as it is worn. Instead of making felt sleeves you may prefer to make knitted or material sleeves. By clever planning you can make felt sleeves (see Fig 16).

The jacket pattern is designed around your own measurement or the measurements of the person it is intended for, eg chest measurement 91.5cm (36in); ÷ 4 = 23cm (9in).

Each panel front and back needs to measure 23cm (9in) not including seam allowance. Work out the shape of the shoulders which is probably a drop of 5cm (2in) from the centre front or back to the tip of the shoulders. If you are making a pattern for yourself, check the slope of your own shoulders by measuring. Cut out the armholes from the tip of the shoulder down below the armpit, this will be approximately 20cm (8in). Cut out the arm shape from the edge of the shoulder to the underarm point where the side seams meet (5cm (2in) will be a big enough underarm allowance for a 91.5cm (36in) chest size). The sleeve needs to fit into the armhole. Calculate the size of the sleeve by the length of the sleeve × the size of the armhole. The size of the armhole is the depth of the shoulder to armpit × two, plus the shaping under the arm × two. For a chest size of 91.5cm (36in) the sleeve will measure 51cm (20in) × the length of the arm, not including the seam allowance. For the wrist shaping measure the wrist and cut the sleeve pattern symmetrically to diminish in width from the shoulder to the wrist (see Fig 16).

To make the sleeve fit the bodice and allow for movement a further panel needs to be cut. This shape is a triangle that fits from the top of the sleeve to either side of the bodice. The addition of this shape stops the jacket looking T-shaped.

The whole shape of the jacket is based on rectangles that can be shaped with tucks, cutting and darts. To make the jacket fit more comfortably and more easily a gusset is cut to fit between the side seams (see Fig 16). The jacket can be made as long or as short as desired. It can also be made longer by adding further shapes (see Colour Plate 21 of finished jacket).

When the pattern has been worked out and made it can be fitted onto the person it is intended for and changed if necessary. Then the felt can be made making sure there is enough for each section of the pattern. Each panel of felt will need to be approximately 51cm (20in) × 61cm (24in) for a 91.5cm (36in) chest. These measurements can be used as a guideline. The pattern can be increased or decreased as necessary. Also the size of each piece of felt can be altered accordingly once the pattern has been made.

Once the felt has been made by whichever method is most suitable, then the individual shape can be cut out. Remember to leave at least 1.3cm (½in) seam allowance. The small off-cuts of felt can be used to make cuffs, collars, and maybe a hat. It is always worth keeping off-cuts as they often become useful. They can be used to make small decorations for the garment you are making, eg buttons or pockets.

USING A COMMERCIAL PATTERN

There is no reason why you should not use a commercial pattern to make felt garments. It is worth bearing in mind that you should look for a pattern that is as simple as possible. Check the pattern does not have lots of darts or difficult shaping. If you can find a pattern with no sleeve seams then this would be quite helpful, but it will probably mean that you will need a very large piece of felt to incorporate the sleeve and front panel in one piece.

You may find it helpful for sizing to use a commercial pattern and you can always adapt the design to suit your needs and add details of pockets, cuffs and collars.

10
QUILTING, EMBROIDERY AND FINISHING TOUCHES

Once you have made the felt and then made
some felt articles, you will need to consider how
to finish off the items. Of course this isn't
necessary if you prefer your felt to remain plain
but felt is an excellent surface to sew into.
Depending on how you intend to use the felt
you may find it useful and practical to consider
different finishing techniques and details.

If you are not sure how you want to finish the felt garments or articles you are about to make, then you will find your samples useful to practise on. Therefore never throw away any pieces of felt, even if you feel they are unsuccessful. A badly made piece of felt may be saved by the addition of hand or machine embroidery. However large or small your samples or cut-off pieces these can be used to try out different finishing techniques.

By sewing into the felt you will be adding strength and decoration. Therefore an item that will get a lot of wear and use will benefit from being strengthened. Felt has a natural elasticity, however well made it is. The use of quilting will help prevent the felt from stretching and bagging unnecessarily.

On certain felt items you may need to add straps for practical use. The addition of other materials needs to be considered carefully because you will want to complement the felt rather than distract from it, therefore it is far better to use materials from the felt making as these will match in colour and texture. If you can make your own braids or your own fastenings this will obviously be an advantage too. If you cannot make your own then you will find a wide range available in haberdashery departments, craft shops and soft-furnishing stores.

Different finishing techniques will be suitable for different items so before you launch into cutting and sewing the felt, consider first what it really needs. Perhaps the felt will need a lining, or maybe it will need strengthening or an opening. What types of seam will be best? You may want to make a feature of seams or hide them inside the garment. Remember one of the advantages of working with felt is that a cut edge does not fray. Therefore you may want to make a feature of an edge rather than covering or turning a hem.

QUILTING

Felt is an ideal surface to be quilted. It is quite springy and sewing into it will give an attractive relief surface. Quilting can be carried out by hand or using a sewing machine and can be as complex or as simple as you like. It is probably easier to use the sewing machine as this is quicker and more uniform than sewing by hand.

What thread to use
When quilting you will need to decide what colour and type of thread to use. You can either use an invisible thread which is like fine fishing line and which will give the felt textured pattern without adding colour or you may prefer to use a contrasting thread so that the lines of stitching make a pattern on the felt surface. If you want the stitching detail to be obvious, you can use a coloured dressmaking thread. On the other hand, if you want the stitching to be more decorative you may have to use double thread through the eye of a needle or an embroidery thread. For extra detail a metallic thread can look very attractive. The best thing to do is to place a strand of thread across the felt to see if the colours and textures complement each other. When you have decided what type and colour thread suits the felt make a small sample. You will only need a tiny piece of felt for this (as small as 5cm (2in) square will be large enough).

Quilting with hand embroidery
Quilting using hand embroidery takes a long time and is in itself a technique that needs to be practised. It is only worth doing if you have both the patience and the skill. Therefore you may find it worth using hand embroidery on smaller items or on selected areas of the felt for a personal touch.

The best stitches to use for hand-embroidery quilting are straight stitch, back stitch and chain stitch. To achieve the quilted texture you will need to pull the thread completely through the felt from the right side to the reverse side. Depending on how you are going to use the hand-quilted felt it is better to keep the reverse side as neat as possible. Try not to leave loose ends. The felt will be much stronger if you tie all the loose ends into knots and then cut the excess thread away. If when you have finished quilting the felt the reverse side is rather untidy you may need to line it with material.

Quilting with machine embroidery
Using sewing machine stitches to quilt the felt is far easier and quicker. You will probably find it neater and stronger as well. Depending on what type of sewing machine you have you can use a variety of stitches. Straight stitch will be the obvious one to use for quilting and this will cover the surface of the felt easily and quickly. If your sewing machine does fancy stitches or zigzag then these could be used instead. It is worth taking the time to make samples to see which stitch is most suitable and looks the best. If your sewing machine has an attachment to use a double-headed needle you could use two different coloured threads at the same time.

One of the main advantages of using sewing-machine stitches for quilting is that the reverse side will be as neat as the right side. Therefore you will not need to line the felt after you have quilted it.

✂ **Plates 49-52** (pages 101-2) Mixing hand and machine embroidery

51

22

52

23

24 ▶

✂ **Colour Plates 22-24** Quilted designs: (top) using lurex thread on a hat; (above) contrasting thread on a bag; (right) cummerbund quilted with machine embroidery

Which design to use

The type and size of the design you use for quilting will depend on the size of your finished product. A smaller item will benefit from close quilting either done by hand or machine whilst a larger item will probably need a larger quilted design. Quilting can also be used to follow the shape of the finished article. For example, if you have made a hat you could quilt the top of the crown with either circular lines of stitching or using a spider's web effect (see Colour Plate 22).

GEOMETRIC QUILTING

The easiest type of design is a geometric one. A lot of different quilted patterns can be achieved with the use of straight lines of stitching. The lines of machine stitching can run in parallel lines of equal distance or at varied intervals and will look very effective. It is, however, important to keep the lines of stitching very straight and equal.

Straight lines of stitching can be made into grids by making lines horizontally and vertically. It is also possible to produce a diamond design by sewing into the felt across the surface diagonally. The lines of stitching could be done with a machine embroidery or a straight stitch. A line of arrowheads will make an effective surface pattern for quilting. Alternatively the lines could be given more definition by using a close zigzag stitch.

To make the quilted design more effective you could sew across the felt with zigzagging lines to make a wavy pattern. For a softer design you could sew in an undulating line of gentle curves. If this type of stitching is used for quilting and sewn vertically and horizontally the finished effect will look very attractive particularly if you use two different coloured threads. Use one colour for the vertical stitching and another for the horizontal stitching.

FLORAL MOTIFS

As an alternative to geometric lines it is possible to quilt the surface of the felt with floral patterns or abstract shapes. If you have made a perfectly plain piece of felt this may be an interesting way of giving it some surface pattern. To quilt in a flower motif is rather more difficult than sewing straight lines, but if you use the sewing machine very slowly it is possible to produce simple shapes and patterns (see Colour Plate 25).

To help you place a design onto the felt that is to be quilted, copy a floral pattern from a picture or piece of material. The chosen design can then be drawn onto the felt with tailor's chalk. The chalk lines can then be followed with sewing-machine stitches or, if preferred, hand embroidery. Depending on the design you may be able to follow the pattern without having to break the flow of the stitches. If the motifs are isolated you will have to break the line of stitching and move the felt around to cover the whole area with the design.

GEOMETRIC MOTIFS

Instead of using floral motifs a series of geometric shapes can be used to make a quilted pattern. A combination of different-sized squares, circles or triangles stitched in contrasting coloured threads would look very effective. The shapes could be isolated or overlapping. Hard-edge shapes are easier to quilt than circles. If you draw the pattern onto the felt first with tailor's chalk, it will make the sewing far easier and will also give you a good idea of how the finished pattern will look.

Following the design in the felt

If you have placed a design in the felt, whether floral, geometric or abstract, it will be interesting to outline the shape with machine or hand quilting. This will make the felted pattern more distinctive and add detail to the finished article. Also, it is easier to follow the pattern in the felt than try and do it freehand.

Freehand machine quilting

If you have a sewing machine that has a free stitch attachment, which means you are not restricted to sewing backwards and forwards, it may be fun to try some freehand embroidery. This would produce a gently controlled abstract quilting and add richness to a plain or patterned piece of felt. You may not want the stitching to distract from the felt and therefore not cover the whole surface with freehand embroidery. Instead you could produce some shapes that are filled in with freehand embroidery quilting. This would be particularly effective when quilting with geometric shapes.

Adding woollen yarn and thread to quilting

If you are using a zigzag stitch it is possible to couch in a thread. The type of thread or yarn you use will depend on the colour and texture of the felt. Any type of woollen yarn could be couched in. A mohair yarn will give the quilted pattern a hairy appearance. A thick yarn would define the quilted shapes boldly. Alternatively, a metallic thread couched in would add sparkle.

When to use quilted felt

Quilted felt will have more uses than plain felt because of its added strength. Quilting the felt for decorative purposes will add interest to a garment or picture and will place definition where it is needed in a design. If you have made a pair of slippers the addition of quilting will prolong their life. It will also help to prevent them from going out of shape.

Quilting a pattern onto a bag will make the bag stronger and more useful for carrying heavy objects. Quilting on a shoulder strap will stop the strap from stretching and pilling too much as it rubs against clothing.

Quilted designs on a hat will help the hat to keep its shape. It is also possible to alter the shape of a hat with lots of machine quilting. For example, you can make the brim stiffer and curved with the use of close machine quilting using straight stitch, at the same time adding decorative detail.

Jackets and waistcoats will also benefit from being made from quilted felt. It helps the garment hold its shape and close quilted designs will help prevent pilling or fluffing of the felt surface. Areas such as elbows are less likely to bag. It is also possible to help a collar stand up by using lots of lines of close stitching.

Wallhangings and rugs may also benefit from being quilted. Quilting a wallhanging helps to compress the fibres and therefore make the felt flatter. Quilting a rug will make it harder wearing.

Quilting a lining
TYPE OF LINING MATERIAL TO USE
A variety of materials can be used for a quilted lining. You need to consider the texture, colour and design of the felt to decide what material would be most suitable, also you need to take into consideration what the felt is going to be used for.

When choosing a lining to be quilted in for a waistcoat, it is probably best to use a thin material as the felt will probably be thick enough anyway. If you are machine quilting in the lining it will need to be a thin fabric in order to get the felt and lining under the sewing-machine foot. If you want to line a jacket with a thick lining it is best to quilt it in with hand embroidery. A suitable lining for a jacket would be silk, satin, cotton or a polyester equivalent.

When quilting the lining for a bag or similar article, it is best to choose a material that is hard wearing and which has a close weave so that no small objects can make a hole and get lost in the lining.

If you are making hats you may prefer to line the inside and therefore quilt the lining in before you make up the shape. If a hat has been made up from a flat pattern it is possible to quilt in the lining on each piece and then sew them together. If the hat is being blocked then it is not a good idea to quilt in a lining as it will not stretch at the same rate as the felt when being pulled over the hat block. Almost any material that is reasonably thin could be used inside a hat, such as silk, cotton, or velvet, or a metallic material.

When choosing a material to be quilted into the felt you should consider the pattern of the quilting you want to use. Some printed materials may have a pattern that you could follow as a design for the quilting. This would look attractive on both sides of the felt. On the right side the machine stitching would pick out the design of the material on the reverse side.

HOW TO QUILT THE LINING TO THE FELT
When quilting a lining into felt you can either cut out each piece of felt to the shape of the finished item or quilt a whole piece of felt with the lining cut to the size of the piece of felt. It is probably more economical to cut the felt out to the shape of the paper pattern and then pin it to the lining material. Make sure the right side of the material is showing on the reverse side of the felt. The felt can then be pinned to the material and the shape cut out.

With the felt pinned to the lining, sew large tacking stitches all the way round the shape and a few across the felt. This will help prevent the lining material from puckering and folding back on itself when you are sewing. Then on the reverse side covered with material, place the piece of felt under the sewing machine foot and sew from the centre outwards. If you are quilting with lines of stitching straight across the felt, it helps to start in the middle and work outwards. If sewing in both directions sew one line horizontally in the middle and then one line vertically in the middle. This will help to hold the material in place whilst you sew the rest of the quilting.

If the lining material you are using is printed with a pattern you wish to follow, it helps to start from the centre and work out towards the edge. There is more chance of keeping the material flat to the felt if you do this. It is better not to pull or tug the material as it may stretch and then you would have tension on the reverse side of the felt which would show when you sew a garment together or place a hanging on the wall. It doesn't really matter which way the grain of the lining material lies because the felt does not have a warp or weft. You should, however, consider the way the pattern of the material will appear on the reverse side.

To help make the edges of the felt and material extra neat you could over-stitch the edges with zigzag, particularly using a lining material that frays a lot. When all the pieces of felt have been quilted to the lining the garment can be sewn together. The finished result will look very neat and attractive.

✂ **Colour Plate 25** Quilted design: waistcoat with flower motifs

✂ **Colour Plate 26** Hand embroidery: slippers decorated with felt balls and embroidery

✂ **Plates 53-56** Quilting in a lining: (page 108) using lurex lining and a flower motif; (page 109) velvet and a grid pattern; (page 110) following printed design on cotton; (page 111) following floral pattern on a jacket lining

HAND AND MACHINE EMBROIDERY FOR DECORATION

Hand or machine embroidery can also be used to pick out particular areas of pattern in the felt and add detail where required. Hand embroidery is particularly useful to add detail that is too difficult to do on a sewing machine. When making three-dimensional items from felt, ie felt balls, it is often only possible to use hand embroidery to add detail because of the difficulty of moving the article under the sewing-machine needle.

Machine embroidery is particularly useful if your sewing machine can produce a variety of stitches. It is suitable when sewing borders and edging details, whether on garments or wallhangings, and can be used to enhance the shape of a pattern on a piece of felt.

BEADING

Another way of decorating the surface of the felt is with the addition of beading. There is such a wide range of beads available from craft shops and haberdashery departments. The choice of colour and type is unlimited whether you choose glass, wood, plastics, ceramic or sequins.

Felt is an ideal surface to be sewn into with beads because of its density. The beads nestle into the surface of the felt and the stitches between each bead can be hidden between the layers of the fleece.

Beads can be sewn into felt that is patterned or unpatterned but can also completely change the appearance of the fabric. Felt can be livened up with beads or sequins. On plain felt with no design beads can be used to make a pattern (see Colour Plate 29). On a patterned felt beads can be used to enhance the pattern (see Colour Plate 30). Alternatively beads can be used to make edging detail and borders. When making felt-ball decorations, beads are useful to make the detail of eyes and other features.

The use of beads to add decoration doesn't mean that the effect has to be bold and brash. Beading detail can be added to look subtle and complement the felt. When choosing beads try and choose colours that tone well with the colours in the felt. Also choose beads that suit the item you are decorating. A small bag will look silly with hundreds of enormous wooden beads sewn on. This would only distract from the felt. Clusters of tiny beads will look far more effective.

Beading mixed with hand embroidery can look particularly attractive. A combination of small glass beads and French knots produces an area of interesting texture and a pretty pattern.

SEAMS

It is very important to consider the types of seam you are going to use to sew felt garments and articles together with. A good thing about sewing with felt is that you have a choice of whether to sew the seam on the outside of the garment or have the seam inside and hidden. The type of seam you choose will depend on the type of felt you have made and the thickness of the felt.

Different items in felt will suit different types of seam, therefore you can either make a feature of the seam or conceal it. Sewing seams in felt is not difficult because the felt is fairly flexible and the cut edge will not fray. You also have the choice of sewing seams together with machine or hand stitches or even using embroidery stitches.

The type of seam you choose to use should really be considered before you cut out the garment or object you want to make. The reason for this is because you will need to allow for the seam allowance. You should also be careful when cutting the felt to avoid edge pieces that tend to be thin and not quite so well felted. If the felt you have made is extremely thick then the seams will be quite difficult to sew. For thick felt you will probably have to hand stitch the felt and use embroidery stitches.

Plain open seams

On most felt articles plain open seams are most suitable. They are also very easy to make. An open seam will need to be pressed open and flat with a steam iron once it has been stitched by hand or machine to make it as unobtrusive as possible. If you are using felt that has a different colour or pattern on each side then the open seam can look quite attractive. For example, if your felt is blue on one side and red on the other and you make the seam on the wrong side, the red side, the blue will show through on the wrong side when the seam is pressed open and flat.

Alternatively, if you want to make the open seams on the outside of the garment this too can look good. If the inside seam has been pressed flat a line of additional stitching can be run along either side of the seam to keep the excess felt flat and therefore make a feature of the seam.

Open seams shown on the right side of a garment are also a good idea if you are using felt made from multicoloured layers of fleece. When the seam has been pressed flat and stitched the cut edge will open out to show the different colours. If you have not used multicoloured layers and want the seam to be on the inside of the garment and to be as neat as possible then it is worth pressing and hand stitching into place.

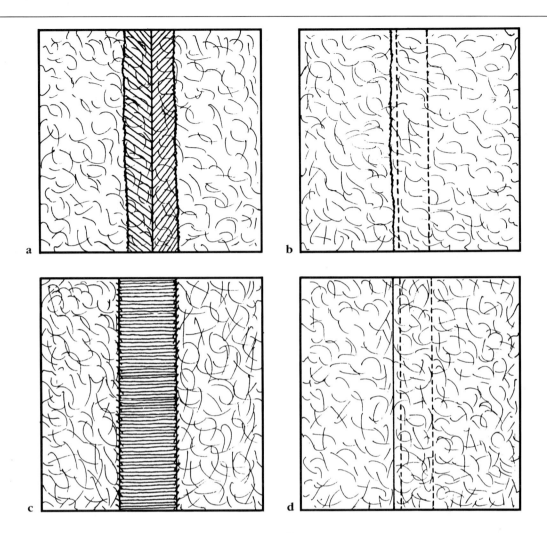

This will make a very smooth seam without drawing interest to it (see Plate 57 and Fig 17).

Fig 17 Seams: a) open flat; b) run and fell; c) covered with ribbon; d) French

Run and fell seam

If the edges of the felt you have made are not very attractive then you will want to hide them as best as possible. This will have to be done on the inside of the felt article. For felt garments with an uncomplicated seam you could use a run and fell seam. This type of seam is particularly strong and much neater than the open seam (see Fig 17(b)).

To make a run and fell seam all you need to do is to sew on the reverse side of the felt a normal seam of 1.3cm (½in) allowance. Then cut one edge of the seam as close as you can to the line of stitching but making sure the felt will not pull away. Next fold the other side of the seam uncut over the cut side, then run a line of stitching close to the cut edge. This will sew the seam flat on the inside and no additional finishing by hand will be needed. The run and fell seam can also be shown on the outside of a garment.

French seam

A French seam is an all-concealing seam. It is usually used for fabric that frays quite badly. However, it is still useful to use on felt items because it is so neat, although you will not be able to use it if the felt is very thick.

To make a French seam you will need to make a thin seam on the right side of the felt but stitching only half the seam allowance. Then on the reverse side make another seam of the full allowance. The raw edges will then be hidden inside the second seam. This enclosed seam can now be pressed flat to one side of the line of stitching. When it has been pressed flat another line of stitching can be used to keep the seam flat and in place. If the felt is too thick to sew for the third time then the seam can be hand stitched flat.

✂ **Plates 57 & 58** Seams and edges: inside flat seam on a
waistcoat (left); bound armhole on waistcoat

Covered seams

If the felt is quite thick and you can only make an open seam then you may well want to cover the seam afterwards to conceal it. This can be very easily done by using cotton tape or ribbon. Choose the tape or ribbon with a width that will cover the open pressed seam. Then the ribbon can be pinned into place and cut to the length of the seam. The ribbon can then either be hand stitched to the felt or machine stitched. The covered seams will make the inside of the garment very neat and will make the seams flat and less bulky.

Using a seam on the outside

You may well decide you want to make a feature of your seams on the outside of the garment or the felt may be too thick to make concealed seams on the inside. Curved seams, such as sleeve seams, can prove to be a particular problem if the felt is very thick. A seam made from thick felt on the inside of a sleeve will prove to be uncomfortable when wearing the garment. If the seam is placed on the outside it will make

✂ **Plates 59 & 60** Seams and edges: feathered edge on hat; cuff detail on jacket showing covered edge and quilting

the garment more comfortable to wear and add an interesting feature.

If your felt is made up of multicoloured layers of fleece then an outside seam is an ideal way to show off the felt. If you do not want to show off the coloured layers but want an outside seam you can use hand or machine embroidery to enhance the seam.

If you use machine embroidery you can use either lines of straight stitch which will make the seam very stiff and flat but pointing outwards, or the edges of the seam could be covered, zigzagged or hand embroidered.

Hand embroidery is the most attractive way to make a feature of an outside seam. There are lots of traditional embroidery stitches that can be used. The seam can either be opened and stitched flat or it can be stitched together to make a ridge. Stitches to use are blanket stitch, criss-cross, shell stitch and over stitch. To add a very decorative element to the seam a combination of different stitches can be used and then highlighted with French knots or beading. If you are unsure which stitches to use then you may find it useful to try a sample on a scrap of felt before sewing into your main piece. It is always worth experimenting first.

EDGES

Edges on felt garments or articles will need to be finished off particularly well otherwise they distract from the main article. The edges should be neat whatever type of finish you use. As with seams, you have the option of either covering the edges or using the felt cut edge as a feature. All the possibilities should be considered. Then choose the way of finishing the edge that will suit the article best.

Making a feature of multicoloured edges
If you have specifically made up your felt from multicoloured layers of fleece then you will want to make a feature of this. The cut edges of felt will open out to show the multicoloured layers but with the addition of machine and hand embroidery the edges can be made even more attractive.

A line of machine straight stitch sewn 0.7cm (¼in) or 1.3cm (½in) from the edge will help open out the layers of fleece even more. The edge can easily be cut with a scalloped zigzagged or straight edge. The felt will not fray so you have plenty of options as to how you can cut the felt. The cut edge on a hat, cuff, collar or belt could be cut with an asymmetrical design to suit the finished article.

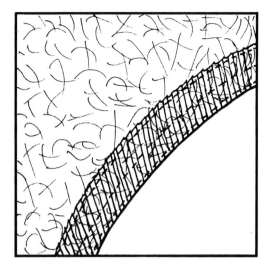

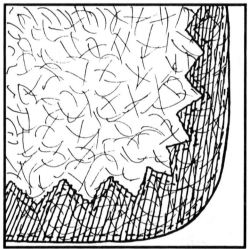

✂ **Fig 18** Edges: plain turned, and fancy cut

Machine embroidery
The cut edges can be very easily finished off with machine embroidery. This could be lots of lines of straight stitches sewn very close together on the edge of the felt or zigzag or fancy stitch covering the edge of the felt. The stitching can be made to look even more interesting by using different coloured threads, either plain, coloured, multicoloured or lurex. Try out different ideas on spare pieces of felt before sewing into the final article.

Hand embroidery
Hand embroidery is particularly useful for finishing edges on felt garments or articles. Hand embroidery is more versatile than machine embroidery, although you may find a combination of the two will be more suitable. The edges of the felt can be manipulated more easily by hand to produce a scalloped edge (see

✂ **Colour Plates 27 & 28** Mitten decorated with a felt flower and embroidery; (inset) mitten decorated with a felt insect and embroidery

✂ **Colour Plate 29** (right) Beading: beaded design on a hat panel

Colour Plate 32). The felt is very easy to embroider into because the thread can be hidden in the layers of the felt as you sew from one motif or area to another. Therefore you could embroider a continuous line of stitching or sew at intervals along the edge.

A covered edge

The neatest and quickest way to finish an edge is probably to cover it with bias strips of material. If you choose a material that contrasts well with the felt and picks out a colour in it, this can look very attractive. The bias width will need to be approximately 5cm (2in) or it can be wider or narrower if necessary. Then sew all the bias strips together so you have a long continuous length of material. With a steam iron fold the strip of material in half lengthways and press with wrong sides together. Then fold the edges inwards towards the centre fold so that the raw edges of the material are folded inside the bias strip.

When you stitch the bias onto the felt article the folded edge can be used as a guide to sew along. The raw edge of the felt and material should be placed flush together with right sides facing. Then fold the bias strip over the edge and on the wrong side you can either hand or machine stitch the other side of the bias strip onto the felt. This will give you an even neat covered edge.

Turned edges

Another quick way of finishing the edges is to turn them. If you consider the turning allowance when cutting the felt you can produce a neat seam edge by folding the felt back on itself. This can be done on the inside or the outside of the article. Depending on how thick the felt is you may be able to fold and stitch and then fold and stitch again, therefore leaving no raw edges showing. Quite often you will find just one fold is enough to finish the edge (see Fig 18).

Braided edge

Adding a braid to felt will produce a neat and attractive finished edge. The braid you choose can either be handmade or commercially made. If you have used braid to make the strap on a bag this braid could also be used to make the edging detail.

It is useful to use braids to finish the cut edge because you do not have to turn the edge of the felt. The braid can be sewn straight onto the edge of it. By careful hand stitching with small stitches the raw edges of the felt can be concealed with the braid (see Colour Plate 31) to give a very neat rounded appearance.

Depending on the type of braid you use it can also be used to give body and therefore stiffen the raw edge.

CARING FOR THE FELT

When you have finished making your garment or decorative object, you will naturally want to look after it.

Felt that is well made is very hard wearing and therefore will last if looked after well. The wool fibre is subjected to quite a harsh treatment during the felt-making process, therefore it is easier to look after than you would imagine.

Pilling or bobbling

Most wool garments tend to pill or bobble. This can be very irritating but it is a natural wear feature of wool. The pilling usually appears where the garment has been rubbed during wear or in the case of a rug, constantly walked over.

The easiest way to remove the bobbles is to pick them off by hand. If the surface of the felt is not decorated by additional stitching by hand or machine, then the felt can be lightly brushed with a wire brush. If you brush the felt you must do it very gently just touching the surface. If you brush the felt too harshly you will find that the appearance of the felt changes and you remove a lot of the fibres. If you want the felt to have a furry or hairy texture, however, then brushing can be used to produce this effect but it should be done before any finishing detail is added.

Depending on how badly the felt has pilled you may find that sticky tape is all you need to remove the bobbles. Take a piece of strong sticky tape and pull it gently across the surface of the felt. The tape will pick up any loose bobbles.

WASHING THE FELT

Felt is very easily washed and can be washed by hand or machine. One thing you must check first is the washability of any other materials you have used. For example, the lining fabric must be washable and not dry cleanable only. Also check that any braids or embroidery threads are colour-fast so that colours will not run when immersed in water. If you have added a lot of beading detail you should be careful when washing. It will probably be better to either hand wash or dry clean a beaded article. If you have used sequins

✂**Colour Plates 31 & 32** (pages 122-3) Edges: cummerbund finished with a braided edge using same yarn as used in felt; and hand-embroidered collar edge

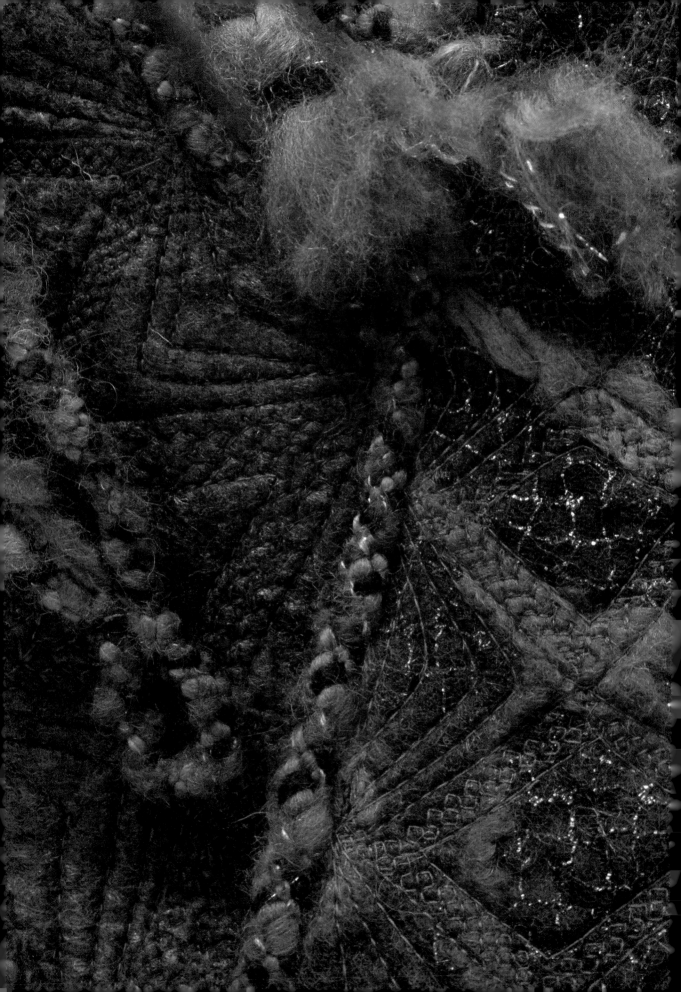

it is better not to wash the article because sequins tend to lose their colour when placed in water.

Hand washing

It is best to use soap flakes or a solution intended for washing woollen garments when hand washing. Add the soap solution to the vessel you are washing in and then mix well with the water. It is best to use cold, tepid or lukewarm water. Make sure to fill the vessel with enough water to cover the felt article. When the soap has been well mixed with the water the felt article can be immersed. The felt will probably resist the water at first but if you gently push the felt under the water it will gradually absorb it. When it is well immersed you should gently squeeze the felt to help remove any dirt that may be imbedded in the surface. Sometimes leaving it to soak and then occasionally squeezing and moving the felt around in the water may be the best way to remove the dirt. If there are some bad stains or areas that are particularly dirty, it may help to place undiluted soap or solution onto the wet felt and then gently work into the felt and leave to soak.

When the felt has been well squeezed and looks much cleaner it will need to be rinsed to remove the soap. The felt article will be heavy with water so it will need to be handled very carefully to avoid stretching. Remove the felt from the water and gently squeeze out all the soapy water. It can then be placed inside a pillow case and spin-dried to remove the rest of the water.

The felt should then be rinsed in several changes of cold, tepid or lukewarm water. Squeeze out between each change of water until there are no traces of soap left. If the article is too large to place in the spindryer or if you do not have one it should be well squeezed by hand to remove the water, but do not wring or twist the felt.

It is best to dry the felt flat as you would a woollen jumper. If the felt is well spun and quite stable it could be hung on a washing line. It is better not to use pegs as these may leave marks in the felt. Pull into shape gently.

Once the felt is dry it can be ironed to reduce ripples and creases that may have appeared in the drying. Depending on what you have sewn into the felt it may be a good idea to use a covering cloth over it rather than ironing straight onto the felt.

Machine washing

If you have a good-quality washing machine with a good wool cycle you may be able to machine wash the felt. As with hand washing you should check that any other materials you have are shrink-proof and colour-fast.

A liquid soap should be used in the washing machine and the felt will probably benefit from being placed inside a pillow case to protect it as it tumbles around in the machine. The felt can also be spun dry in the pillow case and then dried as with the hand-wash procedure.

Dry cleaning

There are different types of dry cleaning methods. If you take your felt to a dry cleaner's either hand in a sample to try or make sure a method will be used that is suitable for felt. A dry cleaner will need to know what fibres and other materials have been used in the felt. He will be able to press it for you but may ask for beads or buttons to be removed. Therefore you may find it easier to hand or machine wash your felt.

APPENDIX:
USEFUL TIPS

You will probably find that you pick up useful advice when speaking to other felt makers. Felt makers usually find their own way of making felt that suits them. This may be a method they have been taught or a method they have developed themselves. Whether you use the hand-rolling method or a washing machine or a felt-making machine, it always helps to talk to other felt makers. Different types of fleece will need different preparations depending on what type of felt you are making. One technique may work better than another for a certain type of fleece.

The technique for hand rolling described in this book has been developed to help produce a smooth felt with a controlled pattern. Other techniques will produce a well-made felt but the pattern that is produced on the felt may be dictated by the felting technique. Therefore you are not in control but the technique is. This can be an interesting way to work if you are not trying to produce defined patterns. This is why it is worth trying out lots of different ways to make your felt.

VARIATION ON THE HAND-ROLLING METHOD

Equipment

Jug	Long rolling pin
Plant gravel tray	Washing-up bowl
Potato masher	Rubber gloves
Kettle	Apron

Boiling water and soap flakes (mixed into a solution in the jug)
Fleece carded or uncarded

Method

1 In the plant gravel tray place one layer of carded fleece. (Alternatively place handfuls of fibre close together if you are using prepared fleece sliver.)

2 Lay out the second layer of carded fleece at right angles to the first layer directly on top.

3 Place the design on the top layer following the direction of the fibres of the top layer. (This is a pattern made from wool fibres.)

4 Hold the potato masher over the fleece in one corner of the plant gravel tray and with the other hand pour a little of the hot water and soap solution onto the fleece. Pour on enough to soak the fleece. Then press down hard with the potato masher about five times. Repeat this all over the surface of the fleece. Continue to press the fleece with the potato masher for about five minutes. Drain off excess water being careful not to move the fleece. (The rolling pin can be used to press the water to one side of the tray and then drain away into the sink.)

5 Add more of the hot soap solution and, wearing rubber gloves, press the surface of the fleece. Drain away cold excess water. Repeat this three times.

6 Turn the fleece over carefully and fold the edges to the centre and repeat step 5.

7 Continue to felt by adding more soap solution and rub the fleece with circular movements in one direction only for five minutes. Repeat this on the other side of the fleece. Drain off excess water.

8 Pour solution over the fleece and roll the fleece around the rolling pin. Roll for ten minutes. Turn the fleece through 90° and repeat. Drain away cold water.

9 Continue rolling the felt and moving through 90° until the fleece is well felted.

10 Place the felt in a washing-up bowl filled with boiling water and leave for a few minutes. Then plunge the felt into a basin of ice-cold water for a few minutes. Repeat hot and cold process again.

11 Rinse the felt in clean water and squeeze out excess water. Hang on the washing line to dry.

NB Use boiling water throughout this method. Letting the fleece sit covered with solution between steps 5 and 6 appears to speed up the felting process. This would also allow you to take a rest!

This technique is used by Carol Connealey. This method suits the felt Carol likes to make because her designs rely on the movement of the fleece. The result is a very soft felt with streaky coloured fleece making a cobweb effect.

ALTERNATIVE COVERING CLOTH

This book suggests that you use canvas, calico or cotton as a covering cloth. The cotton material is very absorbent and sits smoothly on top of the fleece when the water is added. The cotton material also provides a good surface when hand rolling the felt as it holds water and heat. The more texture the cotton has the more friction is achieved which helps in the felt-making process.

However you may prefer to use a material that will not adhere to the fleece at all. As an alternative to using a cotton material a polyester lining material could be used instead. The wool fibres do not attach to the polyester but pockets of air do get trapped between the lining and fleece. Pour on the soap solution with hot water and then gently rub the fleece.

Once the fleece has covered and formed a sheet of fibres the felt can then be rolled. For extra speed it can be rolled up tightly in the polyester lining and beaten with a mallet or be placed in the washing machine. This technique is used by Mary Denham who makes felt slippers. Her felt has abstract patterns formed by coloured fleece.

USING AN INDUSTRIAL MACHINE

Felt made by hand can vary tremendously in effect and quality and it takes a lot of effort to produce a hand-made felt of a good standard that looks professional and is well designed. One of the hazards of felt making is to skimp on the patting and rolling technique and hence produce a felt that isn't well constructed. If the felt is made in the washing machine it can vary in thickness across the surface of the felt and it is less easy to control the pattern and texture.

To produce well-made and designed patterned felt in quantity you really need an industrial felt machine. A few felt makers are prepared to use these because it means they can spend more time designing and dyeing the fleece and less time making the felt. The use of an industrial machine can be very beneficial if you want to produce hand-made felt on a commercial level. A felt manufacturer may be approachable and able to help, if so, you will probably have to pay to use the machinery. It is however worthwhile and interesting visiting a felt factory to see how industrial felt is made.

INDEX

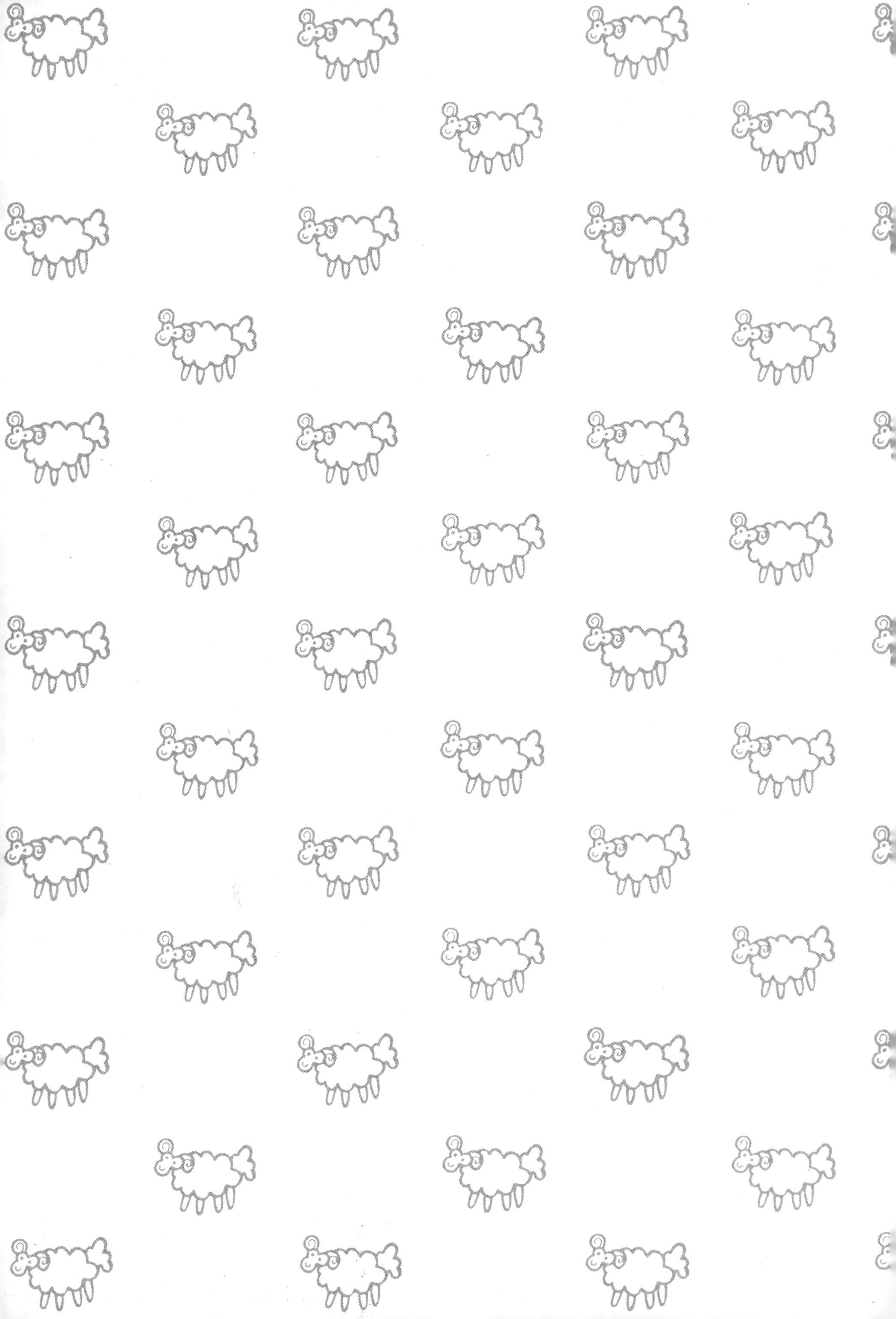